DESTINY'S CHILD

THE UNAUTHORISED BIOGRAPHY

IN WORDS AND PICTURES

BY KEITH RODWAY

FIRST PUBLISHED IN GREAT BRITAIN IN 2001 BY CHROME DREAMS.

A CATALOGUE RECORD FOR THIS BOOK IS AVAILABLE FROM THE BRITISH LIBRARY.

ISBN 1 84240 157 2

TEXT BY **KEITH RODWAY**
EDITED BY **BILLY DANCER**
ART DIRECTION AND DESIGN BY **A CREATIVE EXPERIENCE, LONDON**

CHROME DREAMS
PO BOX 230
NEW MALDEN
SURREY KT3 6YY
UK

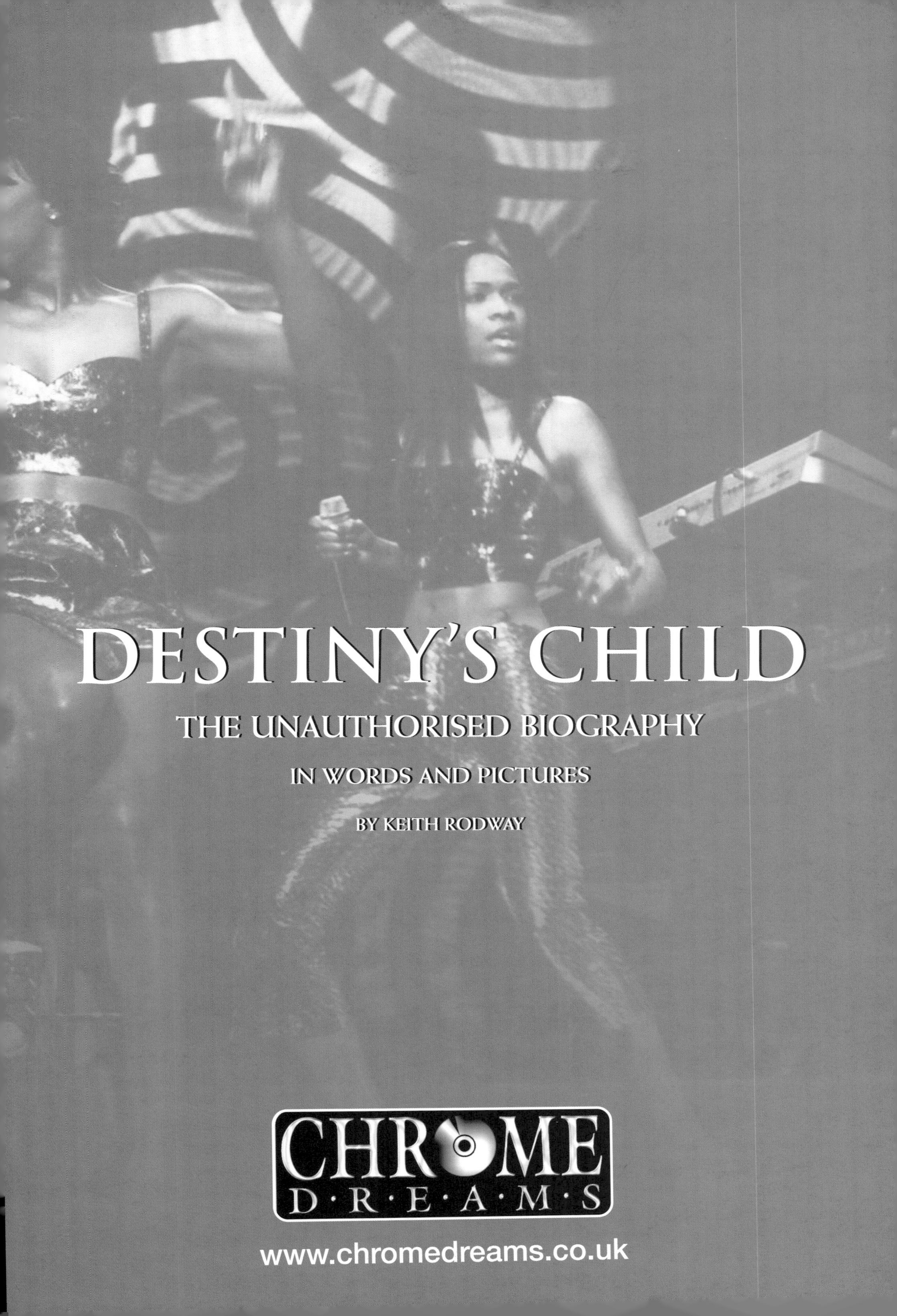

DESTINY'S CHILD

THE UNAUTHORISED BIOGRAPHY

IN WORDS AND PICTURES

BY KEITH RODWAY

CHROME DREAMS

www.chromedreams.co.uk

CONTENTS

INTRODUCTION

A Modern Fairytale

It is generally accepted that in pop music there are two ways to become hugely successful - either through talent or through controversy, but, if possible, through both. Destiny's Child began with the former and have been plagued by the latter, but indeed used both to great advantage. In the process they have turned around the artistic fortunes of a musical genre that had been in danger of becoming stale and overly conformist.

The story of the group's rise to fame reads like a fairytale, complete with beautiful girls leading a charmed life that would seem unlikely if it weren't for the fact that it's all true. Each of the six young women, who have at one time or another been members of the group, possess such sweet, soulful voices that they have earned enviable comparisons with groups such as their idols, The Supremes, initially fronted by the inimitable Diana Ross.

Add to this a unique flair for choreography, driving personal ambition, a loving, visionary family, and an unshakeable, almost text-book spiritual faith, and you have the blueprint for Destiny's Child's extraordinary success.

Their ability, whilst still in their early teens, to form friendships with many of the black music world's prime movers, gave them the chance to call on these heavyweights when it came for their first album to be recorded. In addition, a skillfully negotiated deal with Columbia Records meant that their songs were used, from the start, on prestigious film soundtracks, which have become an essential marketing tool for any young band looking for a way to break into the mainstream. With subsequent releases, they raised the stakes for all those working in the competitive world of contemporary urban music, with their increasingly daring videos, their unique style sense, and, most importantly, their driving, affirmative music, re-writing the R&B rulebook over and over again.

But as with all fairytales, there is a dark side to their story - greed, suspicion, betrayal and disenchantment, leading to Destiny's Child splitting cleanly in half, re-grouping, suffering further trauma, and then going on to become stronger and more successful than ever. And when their troubles seemed sure to engulf them, the intensity of their campaign to dominate the world of global pop music only increased, producing by far their best work to date.

In this book we follow their journey from hardworking teenagers sure of their coming success, to the acknowledged Queens of R&B, who in the process became one of the most influential and celebrated pop bands in the world.

CHAPTER ONE

DESTINY'S

DESTINY CALLING

CHILD

Destiny Calling

Picture this: a warm summer's day in 1991. Two ten-year-old girls, Beyoncé and Kelly, are sitting watching a video of the classic 1960s Tamla Motown vocal group, The Jackson Five. They are in the living room of a nice, average American suburban house. There are signs that the home belongs to a religious family. A warm breeze brings the sounds of other kids in the neighbourhood, playing, shouting, having fun.

Later, down at the hairdressing salon on Montrose Boulevard run by Tina, Beyoncé's mum, they practise the dance routines that they and six of their friends have worked out after hours spent studying the Jacksons as well as Diana Ross and The Supremes. It's the evening, the salon is shut but the girls are at work. There is a tangible buzz of tension and excitement. These girls are not playing. They are already in rigorous training for the fabulous life in showbiz that they have set their hearts on.

Fast-forward ten years. Two of these girls are in London. They are all that remains of the innocent young bunch o wannabes, dreaming of stardom. Now it's just Beyoncé and Kelly from the original group, plus their new partne Michelle. It's a rainy Sunday, and Destiny's Child are playing one of the key major European gigs of the summe season, Jam in the Park in the City's Hyde Park. Soon they will stride out onto the stage in front of an audience packed with adoring fans, and drive another nail in the coffin of the 20th Century male-dominated world of rock music. In the past ten years they have turned childhood dreams into world-conquering reality. They are now the best all-female vocal group in the world, bar none.

Though they may now represent a template for R&B, Destiny's Child are not your average pop band. Their songs combine a celebration of the merits of being young, rich and American, mixed with lambasting the 'dogs' (i.e. males who litter a girl's life with the deceptions and infidelities for which they are so justly renowned. R&B has come a long way since its illegitimate birth half a century earlier somewhere near Memphis. Then it was a raucous and badly-behaved child, running riot in juke joints and sleazy night clubs up and down America. Later, after stowing away on merchant ships bound for places like Liverpool, it jumped ashore and helped re-invent popular music Latterly, it had become largely bland, satin-sheet entertainment, lacking true drive or excitement.

Though veterans of numerous child talent contests and beauty pageants, spurred on by parents eager to see them gain a foothold in the lucrative world of entertainment, Destiny's Child were not pretty-but-vacant showroom dummies. Although equipped for the job, these were no singing models, pouting their way to the top via perfume ads and Hollywood bit parts.

Nor did they come up the hard way, fighting for every precious inch in the grubby streets of wannabe-land, dossing on friends' sofas and eating fries out of McDonald's waste bins. These were sheltered young women from prosperous loving, middle class homes in the leafy suburbs of Houston, Texas. They have made much of their defiantly Southern Christian roots, which they failed to rebelliously shrug off during a troubled adolescence. They are still fiercely devout, often publicly crediting God with their success, and thus following in the footsteps of Puff Daddy and Lauryn Hill.

Compare them to Britain's bad-girl fallen princesses, the now defunct All Saints. Though too beautiful and talented, they threw it all away for a life of partying, shopping and appalling film appearances. Not for them the dignity and flawless professionalism of Beyoncé and her fellow glamazons. They became girl-lads, proving that they could party-down with the hardest. Fashion and hype turned them into the patron Saints of the pretty-but-totally-vacant Big Brother generation, nice but naughty, with nowhere to go, finally, but down, and with little to show at the end of it. In the bad-girl stakes, they reigned supreme, with Nicole Appleton even managing to become pregnant by Liam Gallagher, himself the acknowledged brat-king of the new bad-lads, moody, dysfunctional and at odds with the prevailing spirit of our post-millennial times.

By contrast, Destiny's Child are a mass of contradictions. With All Saints you knew what you were getting, and their street-wise fusion of soul and hip-pop breathed fresh life into the dreary Britpop scene of the late 1990s. But Beyoncé, Kelly and Michelle come over as a mind-warping cross between sexy but untouchable urban she-warriors and glamorous Sunday-school teachers. They may regard the kind of shambolic party-animal behaviour of All Saints as undignified, but when they come out on stage they hit you with such gob-smacking visual flair that you need your jaw propped shut with a crowbar. And when they sing about female independence, you just know that they ain't fighting for the right to wear the waistband of their underwear outside their combat pants. They are declaring war on shallow, fickle and faithless men, with sassiness and spirit that is the natural successor to Aretha Franklin's timeless call to arms in women's struggle for equal rights, 1967's Grammy-winning 'Respect'. And they will win. Of that you can be sure.

So who are they, these glittering tribal queens? How do they manage to rule the hearts of both the pre-teen audiences most usually associated with anodyne boy-bands or syrupy pop R&B, and the minds of self-professed 'serious' rock critics, hoisting the white flag of surrender from the heartlands of a world once ruled by skinny boys with guitars?

Beyoncé Knowles, formerly Destiny's Child's teenage matriarch, now a mature woman of twenty, was born in Houston, Texas on September 4th, 1981. Her father Mathew was once a salesman for a pharmaceutical company. He and his wife Tina set up the hairdressing business. Later, when Destiny's Child became a viable business proposition, he quit his job and became their manager. For Beyoncé, with her father as manager and her mother as stylist, it was very much a family affair.

The Knowles' family photographs show a happy, outgoing child already performing for the camera at the age of six, or smiling proudly as she graduated from junior school. Early publicity shots for Destiny's Child show a fabulously pretty young woman in a combat-style print dress, her smile that of someone who has everything in life to gain, and the confidence to pull it off.

But to get a clearer picture of the background to Beyoncé's early life, you would need to visit the hairdressing salon Headliners, in Houston, where the girls often practised when they were young. These days there are new premises, and with Tina Knowles as the band's stylist, travelling on the road with them, supervising the creation of their extraordinary image, the business is run in her absence by trusted friends and former colleagues.

The salon acts as an unofficial Destiny's Child contact point, with t-shirts in a glass display case and posters on the walls. Fans who have tracked down the phone number ring constantly to get snippets of vital information, such as the way Beyoncé now wears her hair, or maybe asking to speak to Miss Tina, or one of the girls.

Understanding the ethic behind the band's success is to appreciate the close ties that Beyoncé has with her family, and that all the girls have with each other. For many bands a dysfunctional family is a point of reference, almost a guarantee of authenticity. For Destiny's Child, a close family and the freedom it offers are literally articles of faith, as Church and family are inextricably bound together. The local church is near the salon and very often customers who leave saying 'See you on Sunday' are really saying 'See you in Church.'

All three members of Destiny's Child share the devotion that has been a spiritual mainstay for black people in the South for many generations. This belief often reaches an intensity which may seem to more cynical individuals as almost naive, if not in itself an indication of a different kind of dysfunction. Religion and rock and roll have not always been happy partners. Cliff Richard, Cat Stevens, George Harrison, Van Morrison and Sinead O'Connor have all at times been subjected to varying degrees of derision because of their insistence on letting their beliefs influence their music, or their public lives.

A direct route connects the Headliners salon to St. John's United Methodist Church. Beyoncé sang in the choir when she was young, following the traditional career path from church to stage. Pastor Rudy Rasmus is proud of his connection with the group. All three girls come here as often as possible, even when it means getting a flight in, catching the service and flying out again.

St. John's serves an informal congregation who don't 'do suits'. Destiny's Child has been on its prayers list for seven years. Pastor Rasmus is not surprised at the girls' success, though he maintains that Tina and Mathew Knowles would never push their daughter into doing anything against her will. It had always been her dream to perform, to be famous. He has also seen at first hand the sacrifices made by her parents and their protectiveness towards their charges.

For many people, the question of fundamentalist Christianity in America poses problems. Very often it becomes associated with right-wing groups such as the Moral Majority, who often display a distinctly un-Christian intolerance. This air of self-righteous and judgmental moral superiority scares libertarians, and there is much mutual hostility between both factions.

None of this seems to matter to the millions of Destiny's Child fans all over the world. It is the music that counts. The story of the group is a fabled account of ambitious, glamorous and talented young women who invaded the world of pop music with the intention of conquering it. They took no prisoners, and were not interested in compromise. With irrepressible style and panache they won the admiration of millions the world over. These sweet, sassy, sexy Southern belles have seen off any serious competition with a combination of determination, hard work and unshakeable self-esteem.

Rock and roll never had anything like Destiny's Child.

CHAPTER TWO

DESTINY'S

DC

GIRLS TYME

CHILD

Girls Tyme - Lift Off and Beyond

The group began life as Girls Tyme in 1991, when Andretta Tillman, the woman who would later become their friend and mentor, and to whom each Destiny's Child album carries a dedication, auditioned thirty girls between the ages of eight and ten to form a female vocal group.

Among the others who joined Beyoncé in Girls Tyme were her friend LaTavia Roberson, the youngest of the original members, born on November 1st of the same year, and her cousin Kelly, born Kelendria Rowland on February 11th 1981. When Kelly was nine, her mother Doris, who worked as a nanny, agreed that Mathew Knowles should become her legal guardian. Kelly has spent more than half her life in the Knowles family; she and Beyoncé profess to be like sisters.

Fourth original member LeToya Luckett, who joined a year later when the group became Destiny's Child, was born on March 11th, 1981.

From the outset, Girls Tyme began to make a name for themselves in the Houston area. Coming onto the scene when boy bands dominated the airwaves, it may have been that the time was right for an all-girl band to appear. By working hard in voice classes and often spending six hours a day on choreography, they began to shape an act whose sheer professionalism made it hard to ignore. They devised dance moves that were forceful and energetic, and their songs were a vibrant mix of R&B, rap and pop, with the lyrics concentrating mostly on boys and world unity. They learned fast the first golden rule of show business: work comes first.

With this in mind, they quickly built an impressive list of local appearances, like the Miss Black Houston Metroplex Pageant and the People's Workshop's Sammy Davis Jr. Awards, honouring Bobby Womack, which gave the group an early indication of the rewards that hard work and determination could bring. They were asked by Prince to record for his label, Paisley Park, an offer which never came to fruition, and were raved about by the *Houston Chronicle*, the largest circulation newspaper in the area.

A year after they formed, they were invited to perform on *Star Search*, a nation-wide talent contest seeking those keen to gain a break in the entertainment business. A new category had to be invented, as they chose to rap instead of sing. Although they had pinned high hopes on their first network television appearance, they did not win. It seemed that their glittering career had been stopped in its tracks. Three of the members left, leaving Beyoncé, Kelly and LaTavia to continue alone. It was then that LeToya joined them, and the quartet later named Destiny's Child was formed, so named when Tina opened a Bible at the Book of Isaiah and out fell a picture of Beyoncé. On the text beneath was the word 'destiny'; Tina added 'child', and the rest is pure pop history.

Soon after, Mathew Knowles quit work at the pharmaceutical firm, exchanging his safe day-job for the shark-eat-shark world of the music industry. Under his guidance they developed lives a million miles from those written about in their songs. Although they wrote principally about boys, parties, and more boys, their everyday lives were confined to a strict regime of constant rehearsal.

Year in year out Destiny's Child practised and practised. Each summer they participated in the Knowles family 'Summer Camp', which often meant three miles' jogging each day, followed by 'drills' and aerobics. All of them were partly schooled at home. And if they missed out on the usual after-school activities - whether it be going to the playground, to McDonald's or paying a visit to Houston's renowned Astroworld - they seemed to know that such sacrifices would reap their own rewards.

Mathew seemed to have an innate understanding of what it would take for these girls to reach the top. Militaristic though his methods may sound, they have obviously paid off. Destiny's Child is not a group that are afraid of hard work. When they tell you that they have no time for boyfriends, they mean it. For those who think that being a star means turning up, looking pretty, singing a bit, and then banking a fat cheque and making their way down to the car showroom, these girls have news.

In common with many acts on the R&B scene, theirs is an essentially feminine approach, a timely counterbalance to the nihilistic vibe of numerous harder rap artists. In the late 1980s the emergence of the heavily politicised and militaristic imagery of Public Enemy had galvanised rap and hip-hop, giving it a renewed sense of purpose: it was now a war between those who felt excluded from the benefits of the world their fathers and grandfathers had helped to build, and the largely white establishment that wanted to keep it all for themselves. Unfortunately, to the discredit of the whole scene, much of the violence was black-on-black. The anger and alienation that so many young men felt was directed at rival crews, sending out the wrong messages and disrupting the whole process of education and enlightenment. If things in the poorer areas of the inner cities were to improve, killing members of rival factions was not the way forward. As Marvyn Gaye had sung nearly twenty years earlier on 'What's Going On?', 'Brother, Brother, Brother, there's far too many of you dying.' Nothing much had changed.

Destiny's Child and their counterparts in the R&B scene avoided these issues. Their concerns were with boys and their annoying ways. Boys couldn't be trusted, every girl knows that! Central to their key message was their unshakeable self-respect. Aretha Franklin had demanded: 'All I want is respect when I come home.' Once again, despite long, long years of battles between the sexes being fought, with women asking that men show maturity and a sense of responsibility in relationships, nothing much seemed to have changed here either.

As they continued their punishing schedule of rehearsal and local appearances, Destiny's Child's reputation spread wider and their confidence grew. But it still probably came as a huge surprise when Elektra Records decided to sign them up in 1996, when the girls were fifteen. It was five years since they had formed, and had given up whatever a 'normal' life might have been. It seemed now that the hard work and dedication was beginning to pay off.

CHAPTER THREE

DESTINY'S

A QUARTET OF ANGELS DESCENDS

CHILD

A Quartet of Angels Descends

Although Elektra's interest in the group gave them the boost to self-esteem that any act needs when it is trying to establish itself, a resounding blow was not far behind. Hardly had the girls drawn breath to decide how to capitalise on their new fortune, when they were unceremoniously dropped.

In retrospect, Elektra must have kicked themselves. A few weeks later Columbia Records began to show an interest, no doubt drawn to them by the boost to their reputation that their home-town appearances with SWV (Sisters With Voices) and Boyz II Men had given them.

Typical of the response to the girls' act was a piece written in the Houston Chronicle. The writer had met them in a recording studio where they were hanging out with, at this time, no major engagements on the go. At Mathew's suggestion they delivered an acappella performance, stunning their guest and prompting him to write that 'it was an aural collage so beautiful it could have hardly come from four teenagers.' He went on: 'It was as if a quartet of angels had descended from the heavens. Don't be surprised if you see these Houston teens set the rhythm-and-blues industry on its ear in the next few months.'

Fortunately, he was right.

For black people in the southern states of America, religion has always represented a kind of freedom. Following the abolition of slavery, America's black population was, in theory, free. But gross racial prejudice persisted, particularly in the deep South, where a man could be hung for rape if he so much as looked at a white woman. Workers in the region's cotton-growing areas often lived their entire lives on the plantations, where they were relatively safe, rather then venture outside it. Under these conditions, bible meetings or Sunday church services offered the chance to socialise without the restrictions imposed on them elsewhere.

Church communities restored a sense of pride to a much-abused people. Choirs offered the chance to sing, with the fiery and deeply passionate music that came to be known as gospel providing a starting point for literally dozens of the early blues singers. This tradition widened in later years to encompass the soul singers of the 1950s and '60s. Though no longer in the virtual bondage of their parents' generation, many of these young musicians cut their teeth in church. The raw energy of James Brown draws the line where the twin passions of sex and devotion become interchangeable.

So when Beyoncé and Kelly sat to watch videos of The Supremes, studying their harmonies and dance moves, they were seeing sophisticated, urbane young women whose style and appearance deliberately distanced them from the heart-breaking legacy of abuse that their grandparents' generation suffered.

The Supremes were glamorous, sexy and independent, with songs like 'Baby Love', 'Where Did Our Love Go', 'I'm Going To Make You Love Me' and countless others depicting the trials and tribulations of young people living and working in crowded cities, on equal terms with their white counterparts, falling in and out of love, partying and living life to the full. Though not overtly political, they were among the first artists and entertainers who, wittingly or unwittingly, helped move forward the cause of civil rights that would be bitterly contested later in the decade.

It was said that when Martin Luther King was assassinated in 1968, the partying stopped there and then. The bright pop sound of Tamla Motown never regained its former lustre. Label giants like Marvyn Gaye and The Temptations began to pursue a different angle: politicised pop. And when child prodigy Stevie Wonder also began to turn in albums two years later which explored more adult themes than teenage love, it was clear that a significant change had occurred.

In the next decade, the party would be re-invented as disco, when urban culture was forced once again underground, with the agenda this time driven by the sexual politics of the burgeoning gay scene.

Ten years later still, when DJs began playing and repeating only the instrumental breaks in the hard urban soul and funk workouts of such acts as James Brown, Funkadelic and the Meters, hip hop and dance music were born. And with this came a new genre, expanding the prison yard raps of groups like the Last Poets and verbalising the defiance of young men and women caught in the cycle of hardship and misery that persisted in the ghettos and 'projects' of the inner cities. For many, the dreams and aspirations of the generation that had moved north to cities like Chicago, and had helped establish the wealth of such places as Los Angeles and New York, in the fall-out following the depression of the 1930s, had gone sour.

This in part illustrates the musical background of the girls from Destiny's Child. By the 1990s, many black people had built lives away from these intolerable pressures. Black Pride was no longer an underground political faction, it had long been a way of life.

Destiny's Child continues a long tradition. The classic Rhythm and Blues of the 1950s combined electric blues with the horn-driven 'jump' sound pioneered in the 1940s by, among others, Louis Jordan. Later it became part of the fabric of the new soul music of the 1960s, but it remained a category in its own right long after the blues inflection had become almost undetectable.

By the 1990s the term R&B had come to describe the smooth soul of En Vogue, R. Kelly and TLC. Its original nervous rootsy energy had been replaced by faultless production and the genre had become the contemporary equivalent of the 'bedroom soul' of the 1970s, which began with Marvyn Gaye's love anthem, 'Let's Get It On', and spawned a myriad of imitators, including Isaac Hayes, Donna Summer, Luther Vandross and Lionel Ritchie.

So when it came for the group to record *Destiny's Child*, their first album for Columbia, with Mathew Knowles credited as Executive Producer, it was not surprising that the list of mentors and influences reads like a who's who of soul music.

From the first track, 'Second Nature', based in part on 'Make Me Say It Again Girl' by the Isley Brothers, originally part of the Motown stable, whose names dominate the writing credits, it is clear where they are coming from. Rather than sample the original, they opted to re-play it, and from the first few bars you know you're in classic Soul country. There is no hint yet that we are in the heart of the digital age. The guitar licks in, the keyboards swell and then...in come those voices! And at once we're magically transported back in time to the world of, yes, The Supremes and the young Michael Jackson. Homage in all but name, this is classic American black music.

Production on their first album was overseen by Dwayne Wiggins, of Tony, Toni, Toné, who produced four of the album's fourteen tracks. Wiggins first came across the girls before they had signed to Columbia, and was amazed at their professionalism. 'I was just blown away,' he remarked at the time. 'And when they told me their ages, I was like, 'yeah right'. First of all, anyone this good would already have a deal. And no-one that young would be able to blow like that.'

But blow like that they did. Wiggins went on, 'I immediately knew that these girls were going to be huge. They were just like regular teenagers at times, you know, laughing and playing, which was refreshing to see. But they took their work very seriously.'

The second track, and the leading single from the album, 'No, No, No, Part 2' continues to acknowledge the major influences of the past, while drawing heavily on assistance from the heroes of the moment. Sampling the heavyweight forerunner of bedroom soul, Barry White, the track is produced by and features the voice of Wyclef Jean, who came to Houston in July 1997 to remix the song. Fresh from his success with both The Fugees, otherwise known as the Refugee Camp, Jean had also recently scored a multi-platinum success with his own album, *Wyclef Jean Presents The Carnival Featuring Refugee Allstars.*

Already a veteran producer, he had worked with Michael Jackson, Sublime and Britain's Simply Red. By lending his talents to the group's first eponymous album, Jean was confirming what Columbia seemed to know already: that these girls were not to be merely a teenage sensation, destined only to last overnight. These were four young women of formidable talent who had earned a great deal of respect from the local music community due to their tireless performances at hometown venues, and had gathered around them in a short space of time a team of friends and mentors that included some of the best names in the business.

The album continues with a sample of Master P, from 'Freak Hoes', and a vocal contribution and production by JD (Jermaine Dupree) on 'With Me Part 1', the next single, indicating that although Destiny's Child steer away from the contentious attitude of hip-hop on their first album, they are comfortable working with the masters of the genre; the fourth number name-checks Tim Kelley and Bob Robinson of the Funktwons.

The album's fifth track, 'Bridges', features 'replayed elements' of 'Simply Beautiful' by Al Green, and continues Wiggins' policy for hiring session musicians to play the music on the tracks, rather than use a sample library, which many producers are happy to regard as the accepted practise. This organic approach reinforces the retro vibe on much of this debut album.

'No, No, No Part 1', produced by Vincent Herbert and Rob Fusari of 3 Boyz From Newark, is a ballad laid down to sampled beats, while track seven, 'With Me Part 2', features Master P on vocals and is the only track to warrant a writing credit from all four members of Destiny's Child. As they had for Wyclef Jean, who would later be defending himself against claims that he pulled a gun on a magazine editor, the girls had nothing but praise for bad-boy Master P. 'Everybody stereotypes him,' said LeToya, 'saying he's this gansta rapper. But he's not, he's a big teddy bear on the inside.'

'Show Me The Way' harks back to the orchestral sound developed by soul music visionaries Norman Whitfield and Barret Strong in the 1970s, while the ninth track, 'Killing Time', marks Columbia Records' intensive marketing campaign mounted to get maximum exposure for the group right from the start. By the time of their first single for Columbia, the company had already trailed their imminent arrival by licensing 'Killing Time' for the soundtrack of the blockbuster film *Men In Black,* starring Will Smith and Tommy Lee Jones. The movie was one of the blockbuster successes of the year, with a spin-off TV series and a sequel featuring the original stars, due for release in 2002. The soundtrack album found the girls in good company. Among the smooth grooves on offer were tunes from Snoop Doggy Dogg, A Tribe Called Quest and De La Soul. For a band that had yet to prove themselves capable of shifting units, this was obviously a good beginning. Columbia also arranged an appearance at Tower Records with Will Smith, and a party afterwards at Planet Hollywood, where they were able to mingle with high-profile celebrities like Puff Daddy and Mary J. Blige. Thanks to the careful training given the girls by Mathew and Tina Knowles, they behaved like seasoned professionals, showing an understanding of the workings of show business far beyond their years.

The album continues with 'Illusion', a re-reading of 'Just An Illusion' by England's Imagination, briefly a soul sensation themselves in the 1980s. Once again, Wyclef Jean produced and added vocals, with co-production duties going to Jerry 'Te Bass' Duplessis and Pras from the Fugees. Next up is 'Birthday', on which three of the girls get a credit, with LeToya missing out. Track twelve is another cover version: this time it's the Commodores classic 'Sail On', written by Lionel Ritchie, showcasing once more the group's ability to call on the very best of soul music's past masters.

'My Time has Come' is dedicated to Andretta Tillman, who had been responsible for putting together Girls Tyme in 1991, and who had set the girls on their career path. Andretta died of cancer before the album was released, a sad fact that was acknowledged by the group as one of the few downsides of the time surrounding the recording of their first release.

The record closes with an unremarkable pop track called 'Know That', which gave the girls a chance to show off how much they had learned sitting on their living room floor aged ten, studying those classic Motown acts.

With Tina Knowles credited simply as 'hair' in the album's effusive liner notes, the family affair that is Destiny's Child wraps up its debut statement.

CHAPTER FOUR

DESTINY'S

EXPRESS ELEVATOR TO THE STARS

CHILD

Express Elevator To The Stars

Destiny's Child's first major tour kicked off on April 29th 1998 in Nashville, Tennessee, opening for Boyz II Men. In an interview, LeToya claimed that sudden success, far from making them complacent, had actually forced them to work harder, as they now had so much more to prove.

The rollercoaster progress of the tour was later marred by trouble at London's HMV superstore in Oxford Street, where the group were making an in-store appearance. Police later claimed that it was caused by 'well organised disrupters', not by any of the hundreds of genuine fans there to see the group, whose appearance was cut short, ruining the event for hundreds of admirers.

If anyone at Columbia had been worried about how the group's debut single and album would perform, there was no need for concern. They had already supported some of the best acts in the business, and had been given a lot of support themselves by Sisters With Voices. Beyoncé told an interviewer that SWV had 'talked to us about pacing ourselves, and watching out for people who could be hurtful to our careers.'

The fairytale progression of the group continued, and by the time of the first album's release, on February 17th 1998, the single *No, No, No* had already gone platinum, and the remix was a dancefloor favourite in both Europe and America. This may have been the first indication that whatever genre they represented, they invariably came out on top. R&B was established along with hip-hop as one of the most dominant musical forms of the late 20th century, knocking rock music from its perch at the top of the tree, and with the British dance movement finally gaining international acceptance, thanks to artists like Madonna using the UK's premier dance producers on her recordings, Destiny's Child's formula could hardly fail. With a song on a major movie soundtrack, a successful house remix and a platinum single at number one in three leading charts, including Billboard's, what could possibly go wrong?

During the summer months of 1998, the group also watched their album follow the single into the upper reaches of the Billboard chart, finally clocking in at half a million copies by June 1999. Following such acclaim at home, there was equally fervent enthusiasm in Europe, where they spent a week of each month that they toured. Fans everywhere came out in their thousands, packing stadiums and arenas wherever the group appeared.

A new single, *Get On The Bus*, featuring Timbaland, was included in the movie *Why Do Fools Fall In Love* and was released in the autumn as a stopgap between the first and second albums, highlighting their prodigious work rate. By Christmas 1998 they had played thirteen dates in one twelve-day period, and had been honoured three times at the prestigious Soul Train Lady of Soul Awards, outshining their own peers and honoured veterans alike. They had eclipsed Erykah Badu, Janet Jackson, Mary J Blige and Aretha Franklin with their astonishing catch of nominations. During the ceremony at the Santa Monica Civic Auditorium, they were voted Best New R&B Soul And Rap Artist, and the single *No, No, No* won the 'Best R&B Soul Single By A Group' award. Finally their eponymous debut record scooped the top gong in the group category for best R&B Soul album.

In addition to all this, they had been named by B.R.E. magazine 'Best Group of the Year', and No, No, No had come twelfth in the 'Best Song of the Year' rundown on the Billboard chart. This surpassed by one place the hugely successful Celine Dion weepie from the movie *Titanic*, 'My Heart Will Go On'. All this from a group of girls barely of legal age, in the first year of their recording career.

While the album played tribute to its R&B roots, the vocal arrangements on the more progressive tracks looked to the future. It was a formula that would be further explored on their next record and which would come to greater fruition a few years down the line. Though for the time being, Destiny's Child was suffused with the sparkling, uplifting energy that came from the girls' mutual respect and love of life. It presents an ideal picture of happiness: four young people sharing a dream, and realising it through years of non-stop hard work, rarely missing an opportunity to learn from those more experienced than themselves.

The perception of Destiny's Child's music is that it sells predominantly to teenage girls. The truth is not so simple. By crossing over from teen-oriented R&B into mainstream pop, they became respected by fans and hardened critics alike, even winning over the writers of *New Musical Express*, the British weekly rock paper.

In direct contrast to the angst and anger of Los Angeles' and New York's gangsta rap scenes, they brought a very different message to the notice board of city life: that it was the way men behaved in relationships that needed serious attention. They had their own take on life that was non-specific in its appeal. Anyone could listen to their songs, watch their shows, buy their records, become inspired by their example.

By contrast with their first record, which had taken them half their lives to prepare for, the second album took the group just two and a half months to make. In the world of pop music, the gap between records for most bands is up to five years, giving enough time for the market tie-ins of concerts, videos, and general merchandising to scrape dry even the deepest barrel. Received wisdom has it that the first record is the easiest to make as the group members have had plenty of time to write and develop material, and hone it to perfection via all those dreadful gigs in subterranean 'toilets'. With all the subsequent time spent on the road touring the record, not much seems to be left for writing new material, and very often sophomore albums are a pale reflection of their predecessor, with little new ground being covered.

But Destiny's Child don't appear to be subject to the same weaknesses and failings as their peers. Far from having to perform in damp underground dug-outs, they opted for a more dignified approach: find the best and then tour with them. After Boyz II Men and SWV came Ricky Martin and TLC, the latter being their only really serious competition at that time.

1999's *The Writing's On The Wall*, would further consolidate their standing as artists, writers and performers, and was in many people's eyes the place where the Destiny's Child story really begins, with its extraordinary run of chart-topping singles, multi-platinum sales and increasingly sophisticated and daring videos. Having stormed the gates of the citadel, rocked till they dropped and won hearts and minds in every quarter, the group now had to prove that they could make the transition into the more adult world of serious artistry.

CHAPTER FIVE

DESTINY'S

SECONDS OUT

CHILD

Seconds Out

Filling the role that Dwayne Wiggins had occupied on their debut album was Kevin 'She'kspere' Briggs, fresh from his success with TLC on their track 'No Scrubs', which echoed the assault on the male ego that Beyoncé and the girls were now preparing.

Taking the basic idea, from the Biblical Ten Commandments, the girls constructed what might once have been called a Concept Album, in which they linked together the various tracks with a central theme. This was to be The Commandments of Relationships, with each track prefaced by an injunction to avoid this or that: thou shalt not hate; thou shalt pay bills; thou shalt confess, and so on. The title, 'The Writing's On The Wall', is therefore a word-play on the idea of the stone slabs, or 'tablets', handed down by God to Moses, the Old Testament spiritual leader of the tribe of the Israelites.

This time around, the girls insisted that they have a greater share of the writing and production of the album, something that the industry had in previous years discouraged. Women were supposed to look pretty and sing, leaving the really tough decisions to the men.

When making a mainstream pop record the accepted practise often revolves around getting as many high-profile names on your liner notes as your budget will allow, be it 'duets' with other singers - which often means the 'guest' laying down his or her part in a different studio thousand of miles away - or using name remixers to spread the appeal of your product over as wide an area as possible. This can mean that the record you have produced clings precariously to its time and can soon become outdated.

And it can mean that your own input, no matter how great or slight it may be, is lost under a welter of marketing ploys that only serve the moment.

But apart from tracks recorded with Missy 'Misdemeanour' Elliott and Next, there were no high-profile collaborations this time around. All the members of Destiny's Child took a more positive role in the writing and production of the second album, with Beyoncé receiving a production credit on six of the songs. She'kspere himself also produced six songs and was credited as co-executive producer, along with, naturally, Mathew Knowles, who had by now formed two companies, Music World Management and Music World Production.

The album kicks off with a comic routine, with Beyoncé as 'Godfather', her voice deepened to resemble Marlon Brando - the star of the film of the same name made in 1973. The 'Four Families' have been gathered to discuss Destiny's Child's Commandments of Relationships. 'Relationships have changed', declares the Godfather. Then comes the first Commandment - 'Thou Shall Not Hate'.

This leads to the album's opening proper, 'So Good', written by She'kspere, Columbia label-mate Kandi (who co-wrote five songs, including 'Bills, Bills, Bills') and the group. The lead character in the song wants us to know that she's left the 'hood' and is doing 'so, so good'. This is a theme that crops up again and again, not only in Destiny's Child songs but in contemporary R&B and classic soul music generally - an affirmation of upward mobility. 'Make no mistake', sang the late, great rock'n'soul preacher Curtis Mayfield, 'she's moving on up'. With the ghosts of the historic, mythic past at her shoulder she's no time for dealing with the resentment of those who would rather see her fail - 'always bringing me down when you thought that you could' - nor is she making any apology for her defiance and ambition. This is a song of empowerment for positive thinkers everywhere.

'Thou Shall Pay Bills' introduces the first single from the album, the hugely successful song 'Bills, Bills, Bills', later to become the essential anthem of the season.

With its stop-start accents and silky-smooth vocal arrangements, this was a song popular with women everywhere, fed up with having their trust abused by men who start the relationship by pulling their weight financially, but then lapse into a disrespectful dependence, 'maxing out' credit cars, borrowing money until their pay cheque comes along and so on. Perhaps things haven't changed so much since the old times after all; maybe it's something that will never change. But if that's the case, this is one sucker who's having no more of it! From now on, her man pays his way or he walks away.

The song drew a lot of defensive criticism from men who felt that it didn't apply to them, or who simply misunderstood the lyric and thought girls should pay their own bills. In this age of increasing awareness, many men feel that it is insulting to depict them as feckless, irresponsible and treacherous. But the last laugh was on them. If you were not that kind of man, this song didn't concern you! Lighten up! As LeToya explained in *Sister To Sister* magazine, 'The song is about a relationship and the guy is treating the girl really well in the beginning, but then later on down the line he starts taking advantage of her...buying her gifts with her own money. And we're asking him to pay back the bills that he's run up...We aren't saying that you shouldn't help each other out in a relationship. But don't start taking advantage of each other.'

Nonetheless, the song hardened in peoples' minds the image of these dominatrix good-girls, banging the gong in their own favour, apparently having little else to declare than their hunger for money and their self-righteous belief that as God is on their side, they can do little wrong. It was an image that would stick.

The fourth cut, 'Confessions', featuring and produced by Missy Elliott, addresses the need for truthfulness in relationships, while the next track, 'Bug A Boo', returns to the triflin' good-for-nothing type of 'brother', given a tough verbal wake-up call in 'Bills'. This time round they take a shot at guys who expect their girlfriend to just be there whenever they call up, guys who become controlling and obsessive to the point that the woman becomes just another possession to show off to their friends. Well, in Destiny's Child's world, that ain't gonna happen! And the guy is warned: don't think that just because my mum likes you you've got it made!

Feminists had been saying this stuff for decades, ever since the late sixties. And Destiny's Child were not the first to make so blatant a stand in the tousle between the sexes. But many feminist performers of the previous twenty years had been marginalised by an inherently sexist music business. Even when, in the 1980s, hip-hop had stolen a march on the rock-oriented music establishment, it was not long before gangsta rap brought misogynist tendencies back into the front line, with women reduced to 'bitches'and 'hoes'. This infuriated liberals everywhere, who were not convinced by the argument that much of gangsta rap's fury was ironic.

But by the turn of the century, hip-hop had become the best-selling form of popular music on the planet, with the clothes, the attitudes and the language of urban youth culture transformed all over the developed world in the process. By then, it was not just an art form practised by men, many changes had been made. Destiny's Child, rather than being seen as women with an attitude problem, were seen as women with attitude, full stop, taking their message of equality to the top of the charts all over the globe.

'Temptation', which marked the temporary return of Dwayne Wiggins to the production fold, centres on, not surprisingly, the perils of temptation. A downtempo number whose slick backing vocals ooze with suppressed desire, it has the organic feel that Wiggins brought to the first album, with a straight-ahead ballad structure free of trickery or gimmicks.

'Now That She's Gone' is a mid-tempo number warning against 'thinking you got it like that' - not to assume you can come crawling back just because your latest fling has got fed up and left town. The backing is sparse and understated, letting the voices, as ever, dominate the track with smooth assurance. 'Where'd You Go' refines this formula, with Beyoncé credited as co-producer alongside Platinum Status. 'Thou shalt know when he's got to go', the 'commandment' introducing 'Hey Ladies', which tells it like it's gotta be, the girls urging their counterparts in the real world not to let a relationship go past its sell-by date. 'If You Leave' benefits from the presence of Next, his plaintive vocals adding variety to the top line, weaving in and out of the girls' dense harmonic tapestry. The reflective mood of the four previous tunes evaporates as the heat is cranked up a notch for this spirited collaboration, making way for the aptly-titled 'Jumpin' Jumpin'', which became the next single.

Beyoncé gets a full producer's credit, along with Chad 'Dr Cuess' Elliott and Jovonn Alexander. The most infectious cut on the album after 'Bills, Bills, Bills', the song clocks in at a pop-single-classic time of 3 minutes 51 seconds, with ladies being urged to 'git your party on' in its opening 'commandment'.

'Say My Name', also to be a single, produced by Rodney Jerkins, became an instant classic. 'Say my name!' pleads Beyoncé over and over, 'if you ain't running games'. Why can't her boy use her name on the phone? Is there someone else there? Why the sudden change of tone in his voice?

'Thou shalt know when she can't love you' introduces a latino-flavoured ballad, which Beyoncé once again co-produces with She'kspere Briggs, while 'Stay' visits classic 70s Motown country. Beyoncé is credited with 'lead vocal', while the verse's tune seems to suggest the spirit of Stevie Wonder standing at her shoulder. This is classic smooth soul, forgetting for a moment the hurt and anxiety traced by many of the album's previous numbers. As always, the voices are pure, liquid gold, shimmering in the spaces between the song's unobtrusive arrangement and Beyoncé's spine-tingling, impassioned lead.

'Sweet Sixteen', produced by Dwayne Wiggins and Beyoncé, is a million miles from the paean to teenage male lust that its title implies, and is a sweet ballad giving Kelly a chance to come up front and shine, while the group's reading of the classic 'Amazing Grace', providing the album's dedication to Andretta Tillman, allows all four girls to show that all their vocal training and hours spent rehearsing over and over had not gone to waste. This is the kind of bravura acappella performance which had earned them the epithet 'a quartet of angels' in the *Houston Chronicle* just over a year previous. Their friend Andretta would no doubt have been proud of the sophisticated young women that the former members of Girls Thyme had become.

The album closes with 'Get On The Bus', the Timbaland-produced track that gets no album credits at all. This was Destiny's Child's most musically adventurous song so far, with swooping strings and bird calls among the gently rippling bass and guitar figures. The song stops with the line 'I don't really care coz there's no more us', and suddenly the party's over.

Whatever the group's legions of male fans may have thought of the lyrical character assassination they received this time around, it didn't stop men in their thousands buying their records, pinning their increasingly extravagant pictures on their walls and flocking to their concerts.

The album was released on July 27th 1999 and went straight into the Billboard 200 album chart at number 6. With the girls seldom looking the same in any two photos, there was bound to be a new set of images for their second record. The cover shot showed them in white cut-away tops, with Beyoncé's hair in braids. Curiously, only she and Kelly wear a white sash at their necks, distancing them, no matter how subtly, from LaTavia and LeToya. This was the last time all four would be seen on an album together.

By placing an apostrophe in the album's title, a subtle change occurred. If it had been 'The Writings On The Wall', it might have described a set of graffiti. But 'The Writing's On The Wall' implies something different, impending trouble or disaster. If this was intentional, what did it mean? Was it yet another warning for guys to clean up and get with the programme, to stop dissing their women? Or was it subconsciously referring to something rather more serious, a split in the Destiny's Child camp that would come and tear apart the group that had jointly shared the same dream for half their lives? Eight years is a long time to spend with three other people, even if you have agreed that you will be friends for ever and that nothing will come between you.

Nine months after its release date, *The Writing's On The Wall* was at number five on the Billboard chart, having experienced its best week of sales ever. And more than a year later it was still in the Top Twenty and selling upwards of 70,000 units a week. *Bills, Bills, Bills* was at number one on the Billboard singles chart for nine weeks, the same position on R&B radio four weeks in a row, and, together with *Say My Name* it topped the Hot 100 and R&B singles charts. In fact, during the week of October 24th, 2000, Destiny's Child had two singles on the Billboard Hot 100 Airplay Chart - *Independent Women Part 1* at number 9 and *Jumpin' Jumpin'* at number 5.

To promote the album and its accompanying singles - all four of which were number one hits - the group toured in the autumn of 1999 with TLC, who were reported previously to have been themselves suffering internal squabbles. As before, the tour was a sell-out success. It seemed that the group were incapable of putting a foot wrong. With a string of charity performances during the summer, including a benefit for a Houston Comets player who was suffering from cancer, their stars seemed to rise and rise.

With all this in place, they seemed invincible. Or perhaps, because of all this, something was bound to go badly wrong. So, as the uncannily prescient title of the second album implies, there was trouble brewing. It would be their first taste of disaster, and it would hit hard.

CHAPTER SIX

DESTINY'S

FALL OUT

CHILD

Fall Out

According to LeToya, she was lying in bed one morning and the first thing she heard was a DJ saying 'I got some breaking news today, there's a problem with Destiny's Child and I'm gonna give you the scoop later.' It was the first time she had heard it announced officially that the band were having problems. As far as she knew, there were issues to be resolved, mainly surrounding the dissatisfaction that she and LaTavia were experiencing with Mathew Knowles, whose cavalier style of management was making them uneasy, but she assumed that it was a private affair, not public property.

And according to LaTavia, she was in a car when she heard that Destiny's Child had just filmed a video for *Say My Name*, which was surprising for one very good reason: she hadn't been there. So who had been making the video, if not Beyoncé and Kelly on their own. It suddenly dawned on her. There were two new girls in the group. And this must mean that she was out.

With hindsight, it seems unlikely that the dream could last forever. Until the end of 1999, the four childhood friends had worked as hard as they could to achieve their goals and they had reaped the rewards several times over. But both LeToya and LaTavia would have admitted that the intolerable differences of opinion that had built up inside the group could not go on; it was the way in which the situation was resolved that was so hurtful. Hadn't Beyoncé and Kelly always sworn to be their true friends?

To the casual outsider it may seem the two now-former members got choosy about the situation they were in. Mathew Knowles had taken a bunch of teenage wannabes and turned them into global superstars. In fact, the entire Knowles family had taken the two girls under their wing, trained them, dressed them and done everything in their collective power to groom them for their amazing journey to the stars. And then at the end of all that, all the things they had said would happen, had happened. Destiny's Child had far surpassed all the dreams they had held dear for so long.

So what exactly went wrong, when, at the end of their most successful year, in December 1999, just as the new millennium was approaching, rumours began to circulate about a split in the group?

Their music had always depended heavily on its themes of feminine wilfulness and vulnerability in equal proportions. Theirs was not a message written in the language of oppression and exploitation, as had been the case with their spiritual ancestors, the great female Blues singers.

The music industry traditionally loves a winner, but contemporary pop fans are notorious for their short attention spans, and once an act begins to show signs of waning popularity, the fall from grace can be swift and merciless. And the music press, for its part, loves nothing so much as the tantalising scent of trouble.

So when rumours began to circulate that the latest newly-arrived darlings of the pop scene were having problems with two of their members, the group's publicity machine slipped into denial mode, and the press hounds began to gather at the door.

pressure. Sudden success can turn heads, and once-stable partnerships can turn sour where misunderstandings creep in. Unless the problems are spotted early and dealt with sensitively, the inevitable rot begins. With so much to gain, there is far too much to lose.

The crux of the intense falling-out between the combined might of Beyoncé and Kelly on the one hand, respectively the guiding spirit of the group and her beloved cousin, and the relative outsiders (it now turned out) LeToya and LaTavia on the other hand, revolved around allegations of inappropriate conduct by Mathew Knowles. With Beyoncé's family calling the shots on all sides, it was always going to be an uneven match.

Depending on what you believe, Mathew and Tina Knowles are either attentive, protective parents, keeping at all times a watchful eye on the sheltered young women whose interests they represent, or controlling, dictatorial task-masters with an uneven interest in Beyoncé and Kelly. This gave rise to speculation about alleged discrepancies in the girls' wages, with LeToya and LaTavia coming in a disadvantaged second, and about their own lack of creative input, with Beyoncé allegedly grabbing all the best opportunities for herself. And as Mathew was not only Beyoncé's father, but also Kelly's appointed guardian, it was said that here was a serious conflict of interest. Did anyone spot the irony of beginning *The Writing's On the Wall* with a comic sketch about a Mafia family convening to discuss personal politics? For a group that has always professed to be so clued-up about relationships, they seemed to be perilously inept at handling their own.

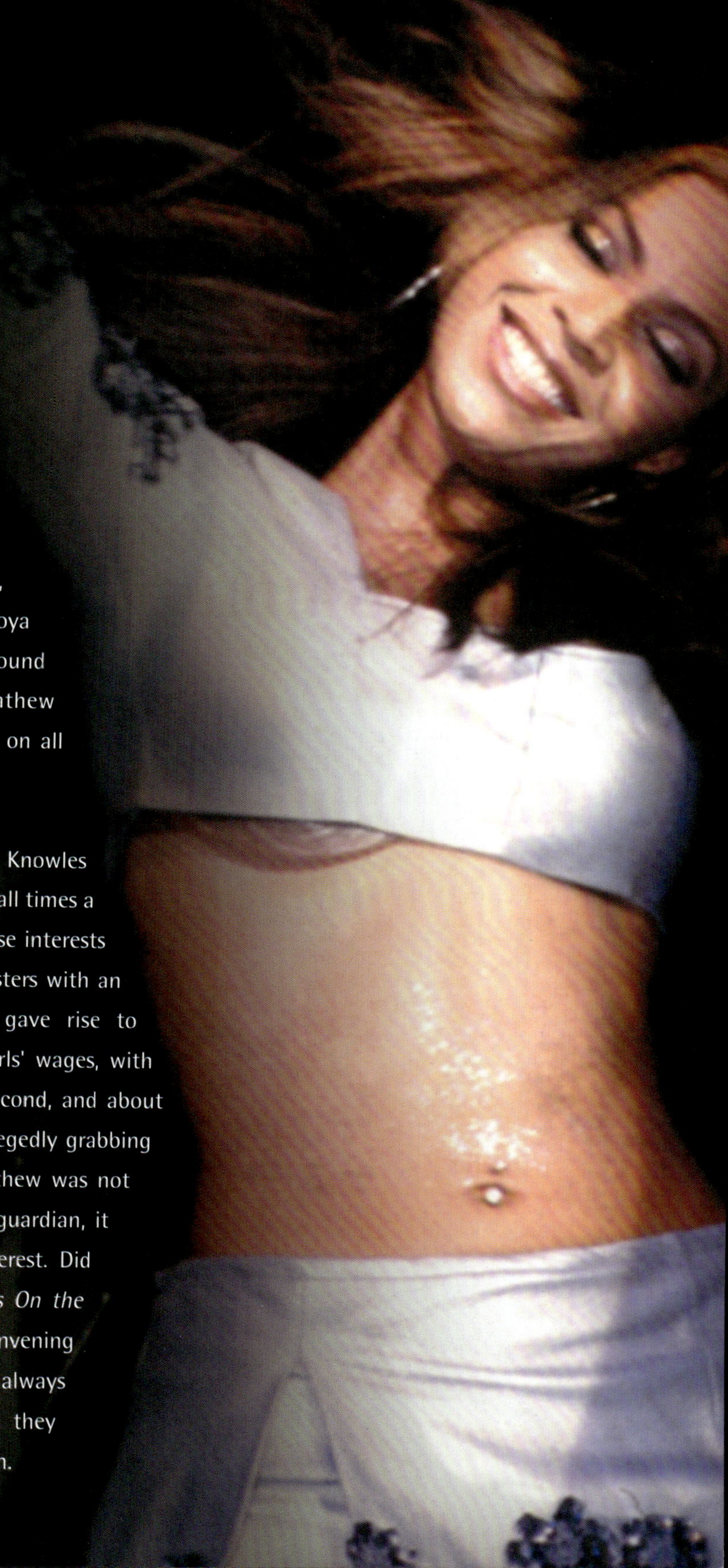

In interview, LaTavia pointed out that, bearing in mind the fact that Mathew Knowles had such a strong interest in the welfare of his daughter and his legal ward, it was bound to happen that she and LeToya would at some time want their own manager, to act on their behalf in a similar fashion. And if it wasn't going to be Mathew Knowles, clearly it had to be someone else. The problem was no one else was welcome.

That seems to have been their big mistake. First of all, they were at fault for noticing that there seemed to be a two-tier system at work in Music World Management; secondly, they had the audacity to seek to do something about it. All this might be all right if the bonds between the girls had survived the rapid rise of the group, but it seems that their vows to love each other as sisters to the glorious end floundered badly in the cold, harsh light of reality. With their respective individual traits advancing at a beyond-normal rate, boiling under the pressure-cooker intensity of lives lived constantly in the limelight, it might now seem obvious that the most dominant personalities in and around the group were always going to want to get their own way, particularly if they were contributing the most to the group's success. Insert here 'Mathew' and 'Beyoncé', and you begin to get the picture.

The two crucial words here seem to be rooted deep in that phrase so familiar in any story about recording artists: 'control freak'. Mathew Knowles is allegedly so controlling that, to paraphrase one anecdote, he would kick God Almighty himself into touch if he wasn't pulling his weight. And then there are comparisons between life in Destiny's Child and the fortunes of others who have been in a similar situation; just ask Mary Wilson what it was like being one of the 'other' Supremes, having to deal on a daily basis with Diana Ross.

But all this is hearsay. No-one except LaTavia and LeToya know what their lives were like in the group, and in interview they are careful to stress that they had no problem at all with Beyoncé or Kelly; and since their lawsuits against Mathew Knowles were settled out of court, they seem to have disappeared from view almost entirely. Unfortunately for them, no-one seems that much interested in former members of Destiny's Child, particularly when the re-formed group is going stronger than ever without them. In the cruel but immortal words of Mick Jagger, who knows a thing or two about the vagaries of fame himself, 'Who wants yesterday's papers?'

The lawsuits had been filed amid claims that Mathew Knowles had taken LeToya's and LaTavia's money, had blocked their creative input and had kicked them out of the band. In a statement to the *Houston Chronicle*, their attorney, Gerald Conley, claimed that up until then the two women had earned less than $100,000 dollars each. Bearing in mind the several-times platinum status of the group, if the allegation bears any truth, this seems in the circumstances to be a derisory sum.

Mathew responded by saying that there had been many creative differences between the group members, perhaps finding it difficult to say outright that the two unwitting outsiders were simply less talented than Beyoncé and Kelly, possibly implying that the assertion that he had acted in a spirit of 'greed, desire for control, self-dealing and promotion of his daughter's interest' was motivated by hurt pride.

It may have been true that, compared to Beyoncé, the creative contributions of the others lacked the depth and scope of the group's unofficial leader, but there are few signs that Kelly was any more proactive than her former colleagues, and plenty to indicate that on the second album all four girls made substantial contributions to the work. Destiny's Child's sound revolves around Beyoncé's distinctive and commanding presence, with her partners providing much-needed, extremely competent and sophisticated support - LaTavia's low alto underpinning perfectly the harmonic structures created by the two lead singers, Beyoncé and Kelly, and LeToya's finely-honed soprano providing equally delicate melodic counterpoints. On the evidence of *The Writing's On the Wall*, it's a match made in heaven, and the girls seem right to have claimed that they had God on their side.

Despite all this, however, it was clear that an intractable rift had formed. While the two ousted members sought to terminate their management contract with Mathew, the Knowles Family devised its stratagem. The retort was swift and decisive. If that was the way the two girls wanted it, they should go. There was to be no negotiation, no group hugs and no sitting around a table discussing alternatives.

Furthermore, in true music business fashion, they were not told straight away, but were left to figure it out for themselves when the video for *Say My Name* was filmed without them, but with the two new members either miming to LeToya's and LaTavia's parts, or having gone into a recording studio behind their backs to re-record them.

None of this behaviour smacks of the caring-sharing, sisters-until-the-end, good moral values that one might expect from such high-profile Christians; but in the end, all is fair in love and war - apparently - and where money and power are concerned, war is often the only word to describe the events that unfold.

For their part, Beyoncé and Kelly were keen to play down these troubles, to find two new band members, and to get these wearisome times behind them.

CHAPTER SEVEN

DESTINY'S

IN EVERY BAD THING

CHILD

In Every Bad Thing

The official announcement came in February 2000, and in interviews made the following month, Beyoncé and Kelly were able to have their say on the split that had occurred. They maintained that the former members had become increasingly disinterested in the group, seeming only to care when their pay cheque would arrive. Their creative input had also been suffering, and they seemed to have become complacent. They would have been right to conclude that this was no way to behave if you wanted to keep standards high and to continue to grow, both artistically and commercially. The last straw had come with the pair's decision to fire Mathew as their manager, whether or not it had seemed to them that they were perfectly justified in doing so. Following the severe breakdowns in communication between them all, it seemed that the only point on which they all agreed was that they had failed to agree.

Five weeks after the official announcement came the news that LeToya and LaTavia were to sue not only Mathew Knowles but Beyoncé and Kelly as well, for breach of partnership duties. By now it had become clear that the apparently smooth transition from Destiny's Child Mark One to Destiny's Child Mark Two, with new members Farrah Franklin and Michelle Williams, had been anything but pain-free. Tense appearances at the Grammy's, where the two exiles found that their replacements had literally taken their seats, didn't help. It was psycho-drama time at Camp Destiny, and everyone seemed determined to give it their all.

In Mathew Knowles' response to LeToya and LaTavia's statement he now made it public that in his mind at least there was a clear division between the front and back lines of the group. 'I can say very clearly', he told the press, 'that there have been no misappropriation of funds and that the two members of the group, the background singers LeToya and LaTavia, decided to fire the manager of Destiny's Child without discussing it with the other members.'

They retorted by saying that they had not left the group, 'despite the defendants' wrongful and malicious efforts to force them to do so.'

'My disappointment,' Mathew concluded, 'is that at the height of these young ladies' careers, they made a bad business decision.'

Farrah Franklin, an aspiring actress and singer, and Michelle Williams, formerly a backing singer with American R&B star Monica, were now brought into the group and immediately introduced to the punishing schedule of twelve hours rehearsal, seven days a week. Neither girl was originally from Houston, a break with tradition for the group. Farrah came from Los Angeles, and was eighteen when she joined the group in March 2000. Michelle's hometown was Rockford, Illinois. When she heard Destiny calling, she was nineteen.

With *The Writing's on the Wall* selling so well, Columbia Records were obviously keen to keep up their campaign to convince the group's fans that the split had been an unfortunate but uncharacteristic blip in the programme.

After the initial round of post-trauma interviews, all press engagements were cancelled from March onwards. When Farrah and Michelle appeared in the *Say My Name* video, fans who had failed to hear the rumours about the split blinked with astonishment at their TV sets, as they tried to figure out what kind of transformation had happened to LeToya and LaTavia.

Otherwise, life for Destiny's Child went on as before. There were, of course, the endless rounds of appearances, rehearsals, video shoots and all the other duties that give the lie to the idea that pop stars sit around the pool all day enjoying the attentions of teenage 'friends' (if they're male) or filing their nails and sipping cocktails (if they're female); or any combinations thereof.

For Farrah and Michelle, life meant a continuous gruelling regime under Mathew's keen direction. What was on offer was a place in one of the world's most successful groups, and that was never going to be easy; what was required was that they give up virtually everything else in exchange.

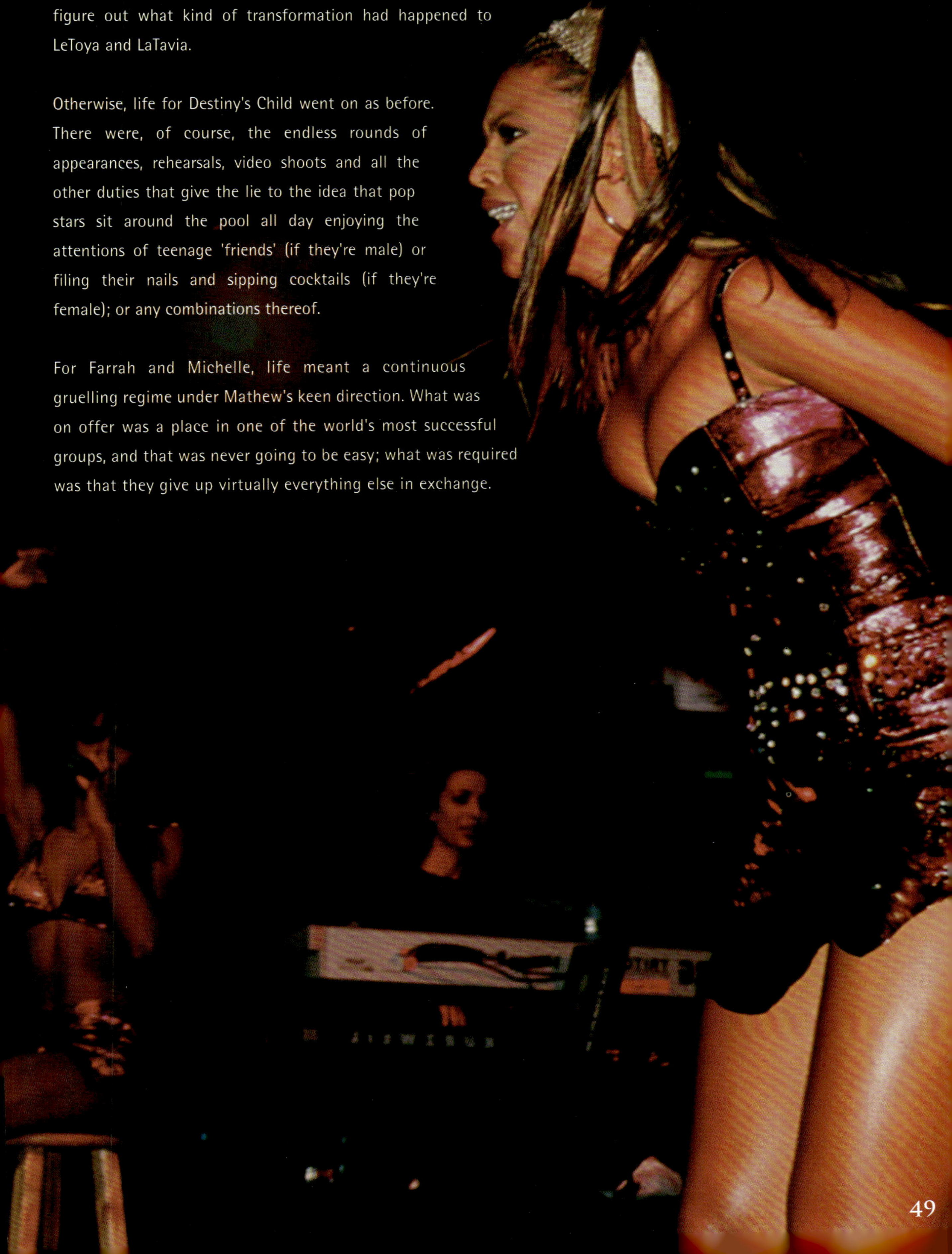

Although *Bills Bills Bills* had earlier been nominated for two Grammys, for Best R&B Performance by a Duo or Group, and Best R&B Song, Destiny's Child were beaten in both categories by their old touring partners, TLC. During the summer of 2000, however, they enjoyed greater and greater success, with the three remaining singles from *The Writing's On The Wall, Bug A Boo, Say My Name and Jumpin' Jumpin'* keeping the album in the Billboard chart for 47 out of the year's 52 weeks. Moreover, the excellent videos for the singles were now on heavy rotation on MTV and VH-1, so any worries that Columbia might have had, proved groundless.

In fact, in true Destiny's Child fashion, the girls claimed that their problems had stimulated their songwriting, with Beyoncé saying that 'in every bad thing, there's a song.' She was keen to emphasise that the mood in the group was definitely up: 'We're very blessed right now. We have the number one single, *Say My Name*, which is a blessing...(we're) very grateful the fans are still standing by us. We've actually sold over a million records since the change, which is a great thing for us.'

'Everybody's been writing,' added Kelly, 'there's been a lot of emotional things going on, I think everybody's been having their pad and pen out.'

She also acknowledged the loyalty of their legions of devoted fans, who had stuck with them through their difficult times. '(They) have been wonderful and, like, every show we've been doing, the crowds are incredible...we just want to thank everybody out there for supporting Destiny's Child still...We're blessed and can't complain.'

With a tour supporting teen sensation Christina Aguilera booked for the summer, the girls felt they needed something to keep their fans interested while they wrote the songs for their next album, their third in as many years. To this end, they recorded the next hit single, *Independent Women,* for inclusion on the soundtrack to *Charlie's Angels*, the movie re-write of the kitsch 70s TV series. The song skilfully wove together the group's ongoing themes of female independence with references to the all-girl crime-busting trio, complete with its line 'Charlie how your angels get down like that', which became an ironic in-joke amongst fashionable cocaine users. With their defiant anti-drugs stance, this may not have amused the group much.

With the song, Beyoncé issued a renewed warning to men to get their act together, and give women credit for their achievements and respect for their self-reliance. Its catchy, breathless refrains reminded us all that this house, that car, these clothes had all been bought with no help from any guy, good, bad or indifferent. This hymn to power-shopping was a massive hit, and revealed a new phase in the group's career - another astonishing upward curve. With its compelling stop-start groove and exultant call-and-answer refrains, this was a great single, with an equally stunning video, proving Beyoncé to be at the very top of her profession, with a group that was virtually unassailable.

There began to be a few murmurs of dissent around this time, however, among people who felt that R&B as a genre, and in particular the music of Destiny's Child, was obsessively materialist, mired in the prevailing preoccupation with glamour and success, and showed an unseemly greed for money. Why was Beyoncé still banging on about paying her bills, and who really cared whether she paid them or not, so long as she and her imaginary partner were happy? Why did these songs give the impression that relationships were merely a business arrangement, and not a mutual exchange of love and respect?

Furthermore, many men now began to feel that the game was getting too rough, with Beyoncé emerging as some kind of furious bitch-queen, hell bent on catty revenge for the wrongs that previous partners, real or imaginary, had tried to lay on her. To some extent, the upcoming album would reinforce that view.

Such reservations may have had their place, or may have been part of the inevitable backlash that always accompanies conspicuous success; what's for sure is that neither Destiny's Child nor their fans seemed about to get hung up on these misgivings.

And the critics who had claimed that the group, having now released three singles with three different line-ups, would not recover from their recent problems were proved wrong. Destiny's Child were showing themselves to be resilient: they were natural survivors. Which was probably just as well.

CHAPTER EIGHT

DESTINY'S

CHILD

AND THEN THEY WERE THREE

And Then They Were Three

Inevitably, there were all sorts of questions raised about the long-term viability of girl groups. The Spice Girls didn't make it - scuppered by personnel and image changes, by the fickle tide of fashion, and, possibly, by the arrival in Earth's orbit of the Destiny Mothership - and neither did All Saints or En Vogue. There were more speculations about Beyoncé, the alleged control freak, now marking time until the next phase of her career, possibly in Hollywood - a singer-actress like Jennifer Lopez, but with better songs. But that was for the future. In the meantime, the group had a third album to make, and the latter half of 2000 was spent touring, and writing and rehearsing the new songs that would be on their new record. And then, in the middle of all this, came the next bombshell to hit the securely reserved defences of Music World Management. After five months of life in Destiny's Child, new recruit Farrah Franklin decided she'd had enough, citing exhaustion and 'dehydration' as the reasons for her desertion. All those hours spent trying to keep up with one of the most tightly disciplined units on the planet - Houston's All-Girl R&B Chart Infiltration Squad - had proved too much for her.

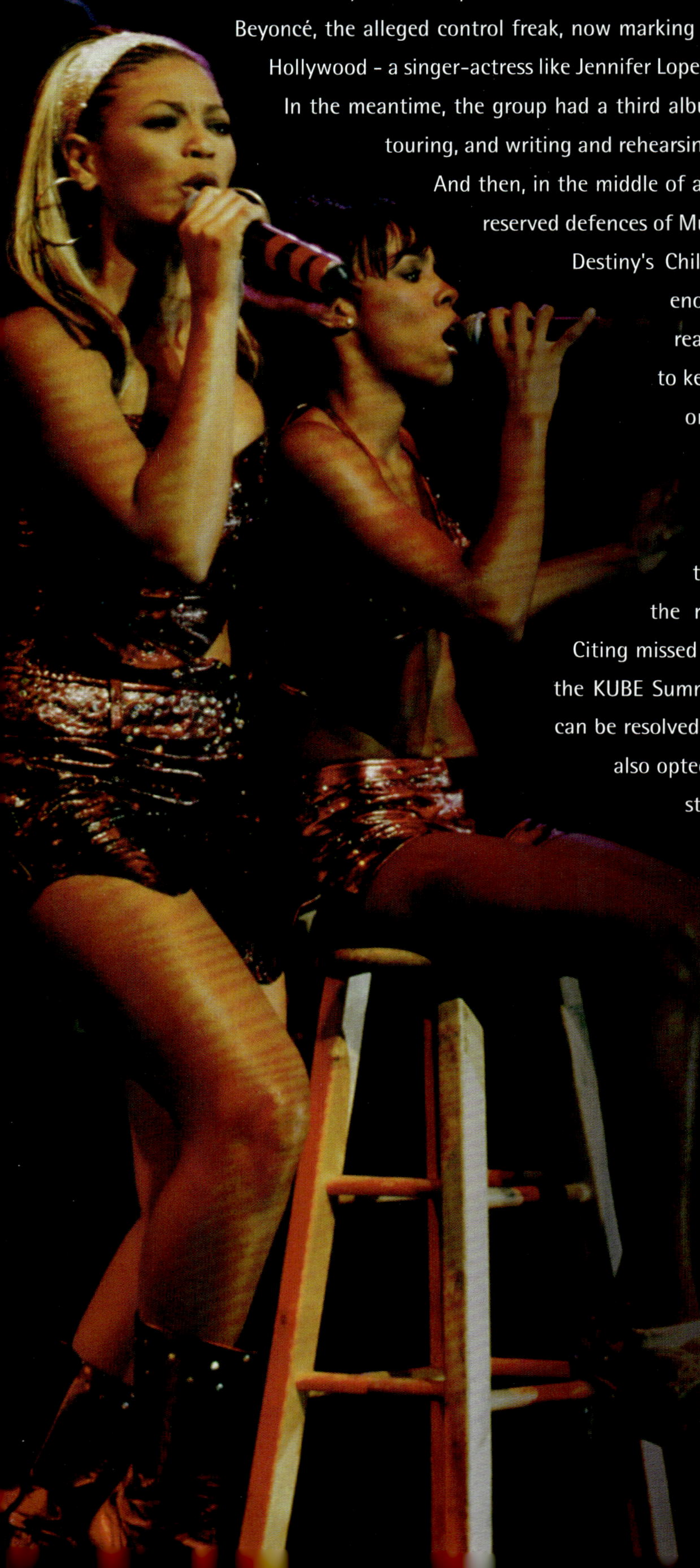

Beyoncé's take on this newest trauma was similar to that on LeToya and LaTavia; they all three lacked the required strength of commitment to The Cause. Citing missed shows, in particular an MTV *All Access Special* and the KUBE Summer Jam, she said that "no personal problems that can be resolved are worth disappointing your fans for". Farrah had also opted not to go on a promotional tour of Australia. This streak of indifference seemed to Beyoncé to be unprofessional. In short, you're either for the group or against. LeToya and LaTavia had been seen to be against; and now so was Farrah. For the second time that year Beyoncé, Kelly and now Michelle - together with Mathew and Tina Knowles - had a tough decision to make. Would America's most sensational hit machine find yet another new member, or would they make a go of it as a trio?

The task of holding more auditions, time-consuming and exhaustive, may have seemed too daunting at a point when work was progressing on the new album and there were always more promotional appearances to be made, new songs to choreograph and new videos to plan.

No attempt was made to replace Farrah. The girls made the decision to continue as a trio. The loss would make no effective difference to the music; the songs would from now on be arranged for three voices rather than four. Michelle Williams had been accepted readily by the fans, and seemed to fit naturally with the two remaining founder members - cousins and virtual sisters Beyoncé and Kelly, who had proved themselves more than equal to the demands of life in the fastest of fast lanes.

In fact, the combination of these three girls has proved to be ideal. As a trio, which in many ways is a classic configuration, reflecting, inevitably, The Supremes, those early goddesses of rhythm-and-pop, they had apparently become much stronger. Promotional photos and CD cover shots of the group in this format somehow look right, as if a balance had been achieved.

Unfortunately, LeToya and LaTavia had always in retrospect seemed to be what Mathew had claimed they were: make-weights, fated always to be literally in the background. They had tried other combinations of personalities but none had been so ideal as this: Beyoncé, Kelly and Michelle. They look positively formidable, these un-crowned Queens of R&B. So two plus two didn't go after all. But if Beyoncé, Kelly, Mathew and Tina still harboured any doubts about the future of their unique family-driven unit, they need not have worried. As the first year of the new millennium drew to a close, the new, stripped-down three-woman Destiny's Child army was regrouping. In many ways, Destiny's Child are the ideal Americans: beautiful, but chaste; talented, clever and hard-working. They love their mothers, God and their President; they don't swear, they haven't done porn movies to advance their careers, they don't do drugs; they are wealthy and successful beyond most people's wildest imaginings; they are modest about their achievements. They model life in the family as a post-modern state of grace, defying the prevailing zeitgeist. They are the Good Girls to hip hop's Bad Boys. Unlike their collective shadow other-self, Eminem, they are not your standard-issue dysfunctional geniuses. There are, as far as we know, no gruesome tales of childhood beatings and humiliations, no destructive relationships with the opposite sex (no relationships with the opposite sex at all, apparently, at least - not for Michelle); they don't advocate gang violence or the use of firearms, they don't do nudity at all, and they don't attempt to glamourise casual sex. They seem to live for their work, their art, their fans. They abhor complacency and lack of discipline. They have no problems whatever with their self-esteem - in fact, if they have any vices at all, it may be the time-honoured failing of sinful pride.

As entertainers they are peerless old-school troupers; nothing is more important than that the show going on; hence the merciless orders dismissal from Destiny HQ issued to any member foolish enough to think she may have it easy: the devil is always at your door, patiently awaiting that vital fateful error. They have been an invaluable part of America's reclaiming of its musical ascendancy over Britain, as twenty-first century British rock bands and vocal groups wallow in a cathartic denial of the riches of the past, reducing their music to dreary, identikit pastiche and self-parody; even its once-groundbreaking dance scene seems to be stuck in low gear. The ravers of the late eighties have grown up and have now got kids and mortgages, and want vacuous homilies where once there were the defiant slogans of the new revolution.

In an interview in July 2001 with London's free newspaper, *Metro*, veteran rapper and founding father of hip hop Darryl 'DMC' McDaniels said that what motivated him now, musically, was the music of Bob Dylan, Pink Floyd and the Rolling Stones. Say what?! Was he joking? Apparently not. He felt that whatever strength and depth British music may once have had, it had been unceremoniously junked in favour of 'fabricated' music, and that the same

Despite this, Wyclef Jean, who himself covered Pink Floyd's 'Wish You Were Here' on his second solo album, *2 Side I A Book,* said when talking on television about the London audience at the Party in the Park of July 2001, that he felt that British audiences were uniquely demanding, lacking any sign of complacency or indifference). So who would save the world from this creeping malaise, this rejection of 'old-school' musical values in favour of the inane junk food for the ears that crams the airwaves, the bars, and the chill-out cafes populated, in Britain at least, by post-ravers who are as likely as anything to be found listening to bland latino 'bliss' music? On the strength of *Independent Women Part 1,* Destiny's Child had cranked up the sassiness knob way past number eleven, delivering a single almost avant-garde in conception, getting up the noses of those who had declared them to be man-hating super-bitches and seeing off any late-comers foolish enough to think they might have even a slim chance of competing in the same arena. In America it was Number One for eleven weeks. Having received heavy pre-release rotation in October 2000 the single ran straight up the airplay charts, lodging at number 9 on the Billboard Hot 100, reaching 65 million listeners, to become their second single on the same chart: at number 5 was *Say My Name,* reaching a total of 75 million listeners. By the time of its release in November it was ready for a straight four-week run at Number One on the Billboard Hot 100 Chart. As if that were not enough, it also achieved a new record in monitored airplay, this time reaching a total of 104.4 million listeners, breaking the precedent set by TLC's *No Scrubs,* also, as has been noted, a song which explores the lamentable shortcomings of the male half of the human race.

Man-bashing? You can't beat it.

If this was a taste of what was to come on the new Destiny's Child album, it was going to be their most wilful work yet. In August the group was nominated, along with Mary J. Blige, for three awards at the sixth annual Soul Train Lady of Soul Awards, including R&B/Soul or Rap Song of the Year for *Say My Name.* Although beaten in that category by Mary J. for her song *All That I Can Say,* the girls came home on September 2nd with two gongs from the award ceremony in Santa Monica - which was broadcast live in New York and Los Angeles - for best R&B/Soul Single for *Say My Name,* and for R&B/Soul Album Of The Year for *The Writing's On The Wall.* Later that month they joined legendary rap stalwart Ol' Dirty Bastard when they guested on basketball player-turned-music star Cam'ron's album *S.D.E.,* whose snappy title expounds the joys of the unholy trinity of Sex, Drugs and Entertainment, all very un-Destiny's-like, apart from the entertainment bit. Other commitments for the autumn included a performance at the *GQ* Men Of The Year Awards, to be held in October, and towards the end of their tour, at Halloween, they were billed to appear at Jam'n 94.5's Monster Jam at Boston's Fleet Center, along with Nelly, Jay-Z and Lil' Kim. Before that, however, on October 5th, at the Magness Arena in Denver, Colorado, Kelly broke two toes of her left foot when she tripped over a backstage ramp during a costume change. Although not obviously the kind of misfortune one would invite, it was to be a break in more ways than one, as Solange, Beyoncé's fourteen-year-old sister, stepped in to deputise for her on-stage, with Kelly herself singing from the wings.

Thus yet another Knowles family member joined the performing clan. Meanwhile, *Charlie's Angels,* starring Drew Barrymore, Cameron Diaz and Lucy Liu, directed by music video maker McG, and whose soundtrack also featured Aerosmith, received its premiere, keeping Destiny's Child in the public imagination while work progressed on the new album. The hit machine's news stories continued rolling out: there were now rumours that Beyoncé had signed a three-record solo deal, with an advance of $1.5 million. Mathew Knowles was quick to refute the claim, but admitted that he was open to the idea of a non-competitive solo deal for each of the girls, fuelling further speculation about the group's future. It was also announced that the new album would be called 'Independent Women' and sessions would welcome back Dwayne Wiggins and Rodney Jerkins to the production fold.

On October 22nd the cable network Lifetime screened a benefit performance in aid of breast cancer research given by a formidable supergroup of female stars, including Beyoncé, Kelly and Michelle, Cyndi Lauper, Sheryl Crow, Ann and Nancy Wilson from Heart, Melissa Etheridge and Amy Grant. In an informal setting, seated on stools in a camp-fire-like semicircle, the women traded versions of each other's songs, and rendered an emotional reading of Paul McCartney's 'Maybe I'm Amazed', dedicated to his wife Linda. The girls also appeared to help spread festive cheer in November at the 68th Christmas Tree Lighting ceremony at the Rockefeller Center in New York, along with Natalie Cole and Marc Anthony, and in December they also sang at Wyclef Jean's benefit concert for his Foundation's efforts to promote musical education for children all over the world. The event was held at the Carnegie Hall and included contributions from old-school rock guitar hero Eric Clapton.

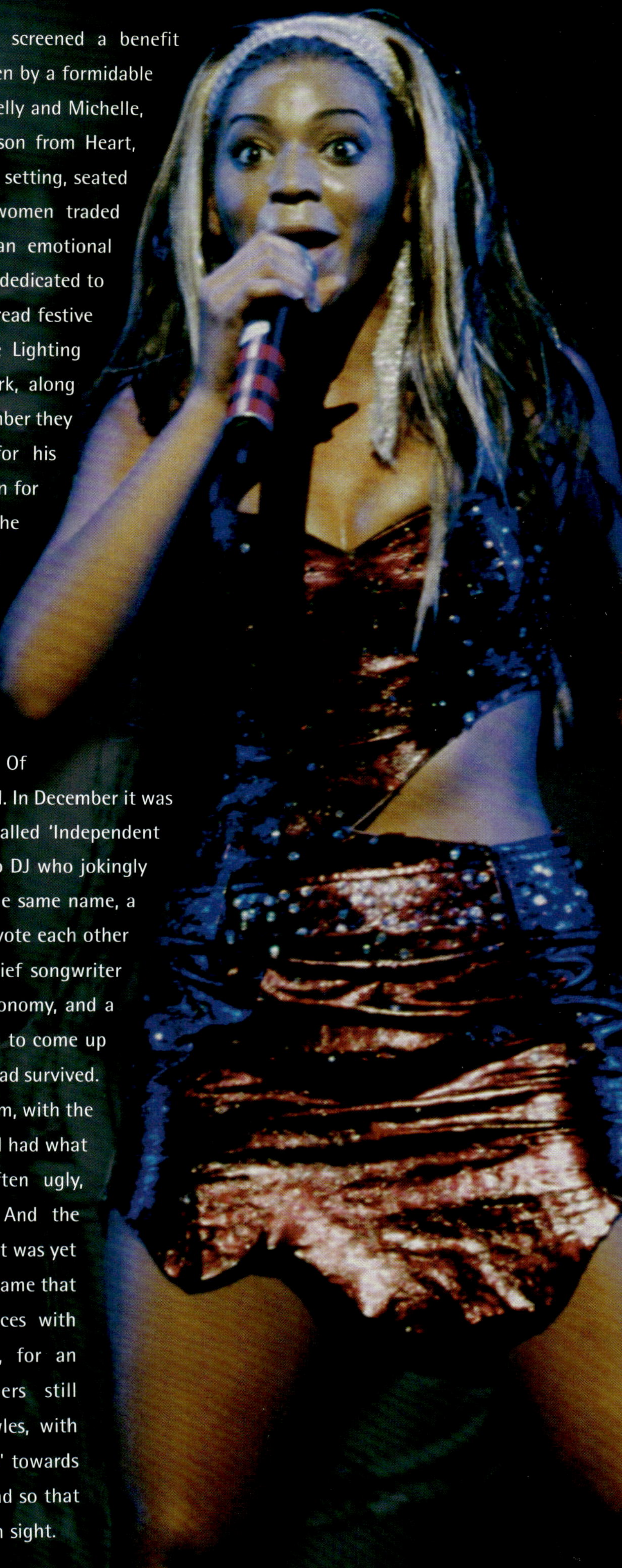

At the Billboard Awards all the top nominees were eclipsed by Siscó from Dru Hill, who came first in no less than six categories. Destiny's Child managed to snap up the award for Artist Of The Year, but otherwise went home empty-handed. In December it was announced that the new album would not be called 'Independent Women', but 'Survivor', a title inspired by a radio DJ who jokingly compared the group to the television show of the same name, a desert island *Big Brother,* where contestants can vote each other off. The album also featured Beyoncé as the chief songwriter and producer, which indicated a new era of autonomy, and a strong evidence that Columbia now trusted them to come up with viable product on their own. They certainly had survived. The past year had been a trail by fire for all of them, with the gods of Planet Pop keen to establish that they still had what it took to really go the distance in the often ugly, treacherous world of global entertainment. And the answer was yes, they could. In many ways, the best was yet to come. And as the New Year dawned, the news came that Beyoncé and Kelly had resolved their differences with LeToya and LaTavia in an 'amicable' fashion, for an 'undisclosed sum'. The two former members still maintained their lawsuit against Mathew Knowles, with the fresh revelation that he had acted 'abusively' towards them, an allegation which he strongly denied. And so that part of the drama rolled on, with no resolution in sight.

CHAPTER NINE

DESTINY'S

AWARDS, AWARDS, AWARDS

CHILD

Awards, Awards, Awards

In the spring of 2001, Destiny's Child visited Millard North High School in Omaha, Nebraska, to play a free concert in the school gymnasium. This red-carpet visit by the Royal Family of R&B was in response to the kids' achievement of having collected one and a half million American pennies, thus winning a charity radio contest. The prize? A visit from Destiny's Child. 'They were kind of a baby band when the offer came to us,' said the school's principal, Linda Wyatt. 'Since then, they've been on all those award shows and so our kids are really excited.'

Beamed down from the DC-3 Mothership, the group treated the children to what must have been one of the most extraordinary experiences of their lives. Here, where the school football team would practise as usual two hours later, the group gave a forty-five minute run through of their faultlessly disciplined stage show, the kids ominously silent and slack-jawed. Then, suddenly, they're gone again, back on their intergalactic tour bus. And the kids go back to their classes, star-shocked and glassy-eyed.

Any other group might not have bothered. As the school principal had said, the appearance was agreed when they were comparatively little-known, and they would have had the opportunity to gracefully decline, on the grounds that they were now too busy.

But principles are essential to the collective outlook of Destiny's Child, and, for all their fame and megastar profile, they have managed so far to remain down to earth and unspoilt. They laugh and cry like other young women of their age, are excited when something good happens, and get down when the news is bad. They like to eat, and have to watch their figures when it comes to photo-shoots. They are both high-velocity goddesses, unattainable and remote, and at the same time just three girls from down-home backgrounds who take time out to honour their commitments. When, later in the year, they gave $500,000 to their local church, they did it because they wanted to, not because it was a another cynically-motivated photo opportunity, a chance to appear grand and munificent. Politicians would do well to learn from this.

Awards ceremonies are nature's way of letting record companies congratulate themselves and their artists for excellence and industry performance, i.e. sales. Everyone likes a party or another chance to show off the spoils of their latest shopping spree - their clothes, their jewellery, their latest fling. They also make for good television, with their high quota of freshly-polished celebrities, their dramas, delights and disappointments; and of course they boost sales, reminding a public possibly fazed by choice fatigue of the many sensible ways to spend their hard-earned dollars.

But however much fun awards ceremonies may be, they are only fluff, and to take them too seriously would be a mistake. The hard task is to keep the quality control button to hand and to remember to press it each time there's a lapse in concentration, to remind who you are and what you're supposed to be doing.

At the American Music Awards in the January of 2001, the girls picked up another gong for Favourite Band, Duo or Group, and the news also came through that, inevitably it seems, the group had been nominated, along with Dr Dre, in five categories for the year's coming Grammys. Dre's latest album, coincidentally titled *2001*, had actually been released at the end of 1999. Though not setting the charts alight at the time, it had gradually proved itself over the following twelve months.

In many ways, the Grammys are the industry's most prestigious bash. Beyoncé (who got her own nomination as songwriter), Kelly and Michelle were competing against a comprehensive directory of pop musicians, past and present, with veteran Quality Rock geeks Steely Dan, former folkie and world music champion Paul Simon, and current leaders of their respective packs, Beck (who had recently come out as a Scientologist), Slipknot, Eminem and Radiohead, all on the nominees list. Ironically, former band members LeToya and LaTavia had also received nominations, as co-writers of 'Say My Name', nominated for Song of the Year and Best R&B Song. While promising that there would be no repeat of the previous year's fraught dramas, Beyoncé acknowledged that the two former members 'had definitely earned' their nominations. If you help write a song, you help write it, she said, but qualified it by saying that you only had to write 'two or three' words to get a credit.

Towards the end of January the group helped give an inauguration concert for George W. Bush, as he moved into the White House to begin his first term of office. Also performing were fellow Texans ZZ Top and Lyle Lovett. By now eleven of thirteen tracks which were intended for *Survivor* had been completed. The album was later expanded to contain eighteen songs in all, with Beyoncé heavily involved in every aspect of its production, and with much of its content said to be inspired by the 'turmoil' the group had suffered during the previous twelve months. 'The year 2000 was very challenging,' said Kelly, 'and I know that gave Beyoncé a lot of inspiration to write songs for the album.' Described as 'diverse and inspiring', the record was one of the most eagerly anticipated releases of the year.

As the awards season continued, the girls picked up a further five nominations for the 7th Annual Blockbuster Entertainment Awards, being nominated in the now-familiar categories, Favourite Group Of The Year and Favourite R&B Group, as well as three nominations in the internet-voting-only categories, Favourite Single *(Say My Name)*, Favourite Song From a Movie *(Independent Women)* and Favourite Group (Pop).

But possibly their most famed award appearance would come the following month, when they appeared at the Brit Awards, the determinedly eccentric gong-fest of the British music industry, and flattened the competition of any kind with a mind-boggling performance of 'Independent Women' that was unlikely to be bettered by any group on the planet, neatly trashing the Brits' somewhat precious idea that to be British is some kind of guarantee of quality.

Beyoncé's own personal star continued its upward curve when it was confirmed that she had been selected to play the role of the eponymous heroine in a 'hip-hopera' up-date of George Bizet's 1875 opera, *Carmen.* She would join Mos Def, Lil Bow Wow and Jermaine Dupree in the MTV-financed production, which was the third time the opera had been adapted for an Afro-American cast. *Carmen Jones,* a musical featuring lyrics by Oscar Hammerstein II, premiered as a Broadway musical in 1943, and was then made into a movie by veteran director Otto Preminger in 1954, starring Dorothy Danridge and Harry Belafonte.

Remakes also figured in Kelly's release of her first solo single, *Angel,* which was to be the first Destiny's Child solo project. The song was featured in the movie *Down To Earth,* starring Chris Rock, a remake of the 1941 film, *Here Comes Mr Jordan,* (also remade as *Heaven Can Wait* with Warren Beatty in 1978). For once, Beyoncé had been upstaged.

At the Grammy Awards ceremony the old guard of rock and pop had a field day with Steely Dan, U2 and Madonna all turning out for their glittering prizes. Destiny's Child won two awards, Best R&B Song and Best Performance by a Duo or a Group, both for 'Say My Name'. At the Blockbuster Entertainment Awards they won Best Group and Best R&B Group. On February 8th they were honoured with the Sammy Davis Jr. Award for Entertainers of the Year at the Soul Train Awards. And 'Say My Name' earned them the NAACP (National Association for the Advancement of Coloured People) Image Award for Outstanding Duo or Group, in recognition of their validity as role models for young Afro-Americans: the awards are officially presented to those from all ethnic origins who promote 'positive images of people of colour.'

To cap all this they also became the first American female group to go straight to Number One in the UK, with the single *Independent Women.*

News concerning the new album emerged with the announcement that the girls were recording a cover version of an obscure 70s disco song, 'Emotion', originally written and produced by Robin and Barry Gibb of the Bee Gees for fellow Australian singer Samantha Sang, giving her her only US chart hit in 1978. The release date for the album was set for May 1st.

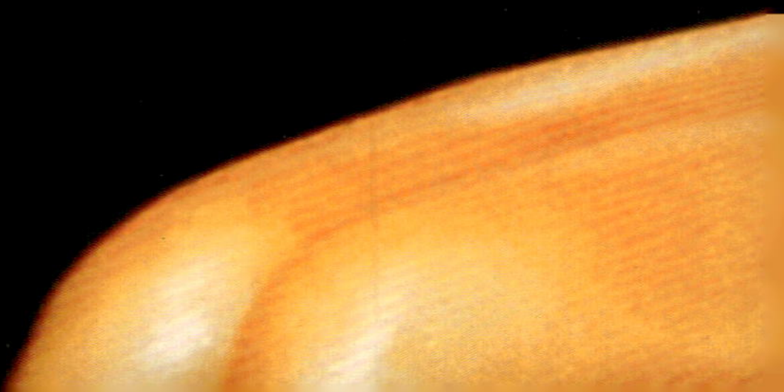

CHAPTER TEN

DESTINY'S

CHILD

NICE GIRLS DO IT IN STYLE

Nice Girls Do It In Style

'No more men-bashing' said Farrah Franklin, when discussing her plans for her solo career, and added that she intended to point up all the good things 'men have done for the ladies.'

Naturally, the 'ladies' at Destiny Central had no such lily-livered plans for their own new set of tunes - rather the opposite. Nor were they about to go soft on those of their own sex who failed to match the mark set by their own examples. And now of course they were, according to the NAACP, officially ideal role models for their peers. Certainly, Columbia Records must have thought so, what with their last record selling 13 million copies.

Survivor hit the shops as announced on May 1st 2001, in all its eighteen-track glory. It was obvious from one glance at the cover shot that this was a new Destiny's Child. Gone were the awkward, slightly self-conscious poses of the former two albums. The girls relax in sexy silvery clothing, looking like they're all about to get into a large, white fluffy bed. The cover art screams 'this is adult music!' The transformation from the Destiny's Child of the first two albums is remarkable; as if they knew that this time the crossover process must be complete. Though still R&B, this album is above all great pop music, as timeless in its own way as any of the great ground-breaking pop albums before it. It is a record that will set a time in people's minds - this is the year that the group would break from the strictures of a genre, to become stars in the wider sense.

Survivor's first track was the song already familiar to fans via *Charlie's Angels*. The film itself had received mediocre critical reviews, but the song did a great job of acting as a taster for the new record.

With its insidious rhythmic style, its celebration of all things material - 'all the honeys making money, all the mamas - profit dollars' - it was a big nod of respect to all those independent women who were doing their own thing, apparently doing the right thing, and taking crap from no-one: 'cos I depend on me!'

Like its predecessor, the follow up, *Survivor* itself, went straight to number one in the UK. With the girls dressed to kill in their designer combats, these urban she-warriors on the rampage clearly intended to state for the records their feelings concerning their split from all and any previous band members: 'Now that you're out of my life I'm so much better' begins a catalogue of grievances and their upbeat conclusion, as the group hack their way through the jungle of tears and recriminations, always finding the same sunlit clearing. They have survived! They have come through the traumas and dramatic changes of the last fifteen months and from here on in, it's all going to be different.

Anybody who has ever suffered the break-up of an intense relationship knows well the urge to get the crap in the past as soon as possible, and any sense of pride and defiance you can muster will help. Inside the CD artwork, the exalted beings clasp hands and raise their faces to some imaginary totem - a source of light, inspiration, strength - no doubt, in their minds, this is the power given them by their intense spiritual beliefs. The song itself is a ritual of cleansing, a purging of negative emotion and the baggage that builds up around it.

With its excellent video, and later-to-be-released video remix, this was one of the songs of the early summer. The image of the girls in tropical-survivalist mode seemed to appear in every paper and magazine going, and the song blasted out of open windows and doorways, from cars and shops. Dance mixes, DJ megamixes, house mixes, two-step underground UK garage mixes and cut-ups gave the group a much-needed street cred rating. Once the collector's scene kicks in, with its bootleg cuts and its manic trading in promos and rarities, you know you've arrived.

The second single, and third cut on the album, 'Bootylicious', maintained the muscular, up-beat pace. This is fit music in so many senses: the girls look better, more confident, and more knowing than before, and the video for *Bootylicious*, with its 70s retro references, its cameo by Fleetwood Mac's Stevie Nicks, whose sampled guitar figure kicks the tune off, is a classic piece of pop-artistry.

Celebrating the joys of being sexy, no matter what size, shape, or colour you may happen to be, the song treads the familiar ground common to most of Destiny's Child's major singles, daring the boys to take on the girls. Can they handle it? Can men handle women who refuse to play the age-old game of showing deference to their men as a matter of course, as if they were denied any real agenda of their own? Playful, sexy and funky, *Bootylicious*, released as a single on July 27th, showcases Destiny's Child with all their strengths intact, and no sign of their weaknesses. Mostly it's the rhythm and the voices, locking together with no sign of strain or artifice. Mathew Knowles even gets a writing credit, with Beyoncé getting her name first everywhere, as with most of the songs on the record, as both writer and producer, with co-production by Rob Fusari and Falonte Moore. 'Bootylicious' is classy, and classic, R&B.

But then, with the album's fourth song, 'Nasty Girl', the mood changes and the spell is broken. 'You're so nasty, trashy, sleazy, classless' accuse the voices with an insistent sneer, and go on to make it clear that the victim of their scorn - another woman - has no right to leave the house looking the way she does, flaunting all she's got for all to see. Put some clothes on you nasty girl!

Beyoncé, Kelly and Michelle are not shy about their physiques. We all know they have grea
bodies, and so do they. In the August 2001 edition of *Esquire*, one of the more restrainec
men's lifestyle magazines available in newsagents, which avoids the tacky soft-porr
approach of the dozens of 'lad mags', (i.e., magazines for men whose interests
centre mainly on sport, money and women), the group make the somewha
disingenuous claim that "we do not go out of our way to be sexy." And woulc
they if they could? Or do they just put up with it, like an irritating headache

"We will show skin," they go on, "but we have to feel comfortable. You
can walk in somewhere in a sexy dress but you have God with you." This
is all very well, and another point checked for dignity and pride, bu
does it give them a mandate to slag off other women who wish to
express themselves differently? First man-bashing, now a
sanctimonious, holier-than-thou go at 'nasty girls'.

'Fancy' gives Beyoncé the chance to get more bitterness out of he
system as she tears a strip off girls who doggedly follow you
around, trying to hit it off first with the men who are coming on to
you, getting in the way and just being generally a pain in the neck
Dwayne Wiggins is brought back on board, but this time as co-
producer, supplying guitar in the break-downs, and infusing the
track with his knack of making it all seem so simple.

But then the mood shifts, the gloom lifts and the good humou
returns for 'Apple Pie A La Mode', a tour-de-force of writing
arranging and singing, with all the girls up-front in the mix
the harmonies swooping and gliding like no other group or
Earth. With all the fuss and hype surrounding Beyoncé's persona
and artistic growth - there's no doubt this is her record - it is easy
to forget that Kelly and Michelle provide their soul sister with
such sweet support, always there a hundred percent, like the
inspired professionals they would wish to be. There is never a
lapse of judgement, and no ego clashes marring the flow o
the music. This is tricky, complex stuff, its delivery a perfec
mix of understatement and subtle power.

The song sings the praises of those men who jus
knock you out when they walk in the room
but don't even know they're doing it. Writter
and produced once again by Beyoncé, Rob
Fusari and Falonte Moore, this is the sounc
of sunshine pouring out of your stereo
Get up, slam it on, have a great day!

Six songs in, and there's another twelve to go, and so far no sign of the pace slowing. 'Sexy Daddy', with its fractured ragga style, just wants the girls to have fun - in fact, it insists on it. Timpanies and assorted clattering percussion indicate a less-is-more backdrop, with the voices once again strutting their unique stuff over truly eccentric backing. 'It's the weekend and it's time for freaking' is the basic proposition here, with all the edgy excitement you'd expect. Beyoncé brings in Damon Elliott to help with production, and it's hard to know where the line between her ideas and his is drawn as is the case with most of the songs on *Survivor.* She has clearly learned a lot, and learned it fast, and celebrity producers taking a front seat are off the agenda.

'Perfect Man' (which was licensed for the soundtrack to the movie *Romeo Must Die*) sounds suspiciously like filler. It neither breaks the spell nor jacks up the heat, dealing with the awkward moment when you see a man you think is the one you've waited for all your life, and you suddenly discover you've lost the nerve to tell him so. Zing! go the vibrant strings of you heart, while your brain bolts shut your mouth and suddenly the moment's gone. Helped out by Rapture Stewart and Eric Seats of Key Beats Inc, the beats are in fact strangely unengaging, and the song reprises those Motown-style vocal tricks that the group know they can fall back on when the well of inspiration has run temporarily dry.

'Independent Women Part II' reprises the hit single, with the ghost of Carmen creeping in at the edges, making one wonder what Georges Bizet would have made of the influence on 21st Century popular music his opera has had. Introduced with a sample from a truly wacky piece of music called 'Peabody's Improbable History', by Frank Comstock, this decidedly odd treatment is followed by the pure sunshine pop of 'Happy Face', the most infectious song on the whole record. If you're down, or if it's a beautiful day, or if you just want to feel good, put this on and turn it up. Happiness guaranteed. Skittering along on its sly synth riff, reminiscent of Madonna's work with William Orbit, this is the perfect poptone for the city summer. Wear it and smile. 'Dance With Me' slows the pace, clearing the way for a run into ballad country. This is the sort of stuff that the group can no doubt pull off without having to try. But then comes a strange kind of surprise, a hint at what the future might hold if Destiny's Child ever fragmented and Beyoncé found herself embarking on that solo career...

'My Heart Still Beats', a collaboration with producer and arranger Walter Afanasieff, is a power ballad of the kind that Celine Dion has made an industry; this is production-line adult soul, which, as the liner notes tell us, 'features Beyoncé' (in other words, it doesn't feature the others at all). No doubt intended as a showcase for her ability to carry off a reflective ballad with the same deadly accuracy with which she parades her bigger ideas, it doesn't quite work. If you want this sort of thing, play that Celine record. Or, alternatively, don't bother.

What 'My Heart Still Beats' does do, though, is to show by contrast what can be done when you have a top-class songwriting partnership on your side. 'Emotion', the cover version of the Bee Gees track announced earlier in the year, has everything that 'My Heart Still Beats' lacks. Robin and Barry Gibb have been writing flawlessly professional ballads for more than forty years, and it shows. With this kind of support, Beyoncé, Kelly and Michelle can trade top lines with consummate ease; if those harmonies don't reduce you to submission, your soul is missing some vital component. Co-produced by Beyoncé and Mathew, with Mark Fiest, this breathes new life into an album that seemed to be losing its vital energy. 'Brown Eyes' continues the string of somewhat gloopy ballads, without shaking the world's foundations, and we can cruise through 'Dangerously In Love', it being more or less straight-ahead downtempo R&B, but 'The Story of Beauty' is probably *Survivor's* bravest cut, inspired by a letter from a young fan who had been emotionally abused by her step-father, and who is fighting for survival of a different kind: the survival of her trust, her innocence, her faith in those she loves, and those who betray her; and finally the survival of love itself.

The 'Gospel Medley' that follows celebrates the survival of love after death, as the group pay tribute once more to their friend Andretta Tillman, and give themselves the opportunity to display the skills and discipline they learned singing in church. Sung acappella, it is the first of two very spiritual numbers that close the album. The final track, 'Outro (DC-3) Thank You' is either charming or self-indulgent, depending on how you feel about such public affirmations of very personal feelings, affection and declarations of faith.

Needless to say, the album was a no-holds-barred smash, going straight to the top of the Billboard Hot 100 Chart, and suddenly Destiny's Child were everywhere, with Beyoncé in her long blonde ringlets, and Kelly and Michelle looking so pretty it, seemed almost unnatural. With the summer season barely under way, the group had delivered their manifesto for election to the top of the charts wherever human beings listen to music. Only a major disaster could stop them now, and that just didn't seem to be an option.

On May 8th, the first network screening of *Carmen* was shown, inaugurating not only Beyoncé's first high-profile project outside the group, but also, with the movie soundtrack, the first release on Mathew Knowles' own record label, Music World Music, the next step in the growth of the Knowles Family business empire.

For this latest version of the story, Carmen is renamed Carmen Brown and the action is relocated from Spain to Los Angeles, where the central character enters into a doomed relationship with an LA police officer, played by Mekhi Pfifer.

With all the ingredients of a classic love story, opera style - love, murder, betrayal - and with a stellar cast of hip-hop front-runners, it gave Beyoncé the opportunity to expand her repertoire into straight acting. Already the flow of potential scripts from Hollywood had begun, with offers for both Beyoncé on her own - she had to turn down an appearance in *Men In Black 2* - and for the group as a whole.

The same day saw the release of *Survivor - The Dance Mixes* - a maxi CD single featuring an extended version with Da Brat, two mixes from Calderone - the 'Calderone Club Mix' and 'Drum Dub Mix', as well as a 'CB 2000 Club Anthem Mix' and an 'Azzaz Soul Remix'. The same material was also available on vinyl.

In *The New York Times* the ambitious production was described as "an audacious blend of drama, hip-hop, movie musicals and visual flash...the artistically sophisticated *Carmen* may be the most mature film MTV has yet produced."

Beyoncé herself remarked 'I know the film *(Carmen Jones)* is legendary, and it's hard to touch things like that. Hopefully, people our age and our generation will be interested to see that classic story retold.'

The soundtrack featured several Destiny's Child-related re-workings and new collaborations. *Survivor's* remix by Da Brat appeared again, while 'Bootylicious', featuring Missy Elliott, was given a new treatment, the 'Rockwilder' remix. Beyoncé also appeared in two new trio settings: on 'Cards Never Lie', with Wyclef Jean and Rah Digga, and with Mos Def and Sam Sarpong on 'If Looks Could Kill You Would Be Dead.'

Meanwhile, there was news of former members of the group. Farrah Franklin was planning a solo project and was writing demos for it, whilst also planning 'a calendar and possibly a book', and LeToya and LaTavia were forming a group, along with an unnamed third member, called Angel. None of this, of course, would make the slightest difference to the girls, who announced on the eve of the release of *Survivor* that they would be headlining a new

MTV project, the TRL (Total Request Live) Tour, which would start in the US in July and would visit thirty cities.

More world domination strategies would no doubt emerge once the record was in the shops, with its sights set squarely once more on the hearts and pockets of millions the world over.

CHAPTER ELEVEN

DESTINY'S

CHILD

QUEENS OF R&B

All Hail The Queens Of R&B

Even the *NME* had been impressed.

The *New Musical Express*, the weekly British rock paper that is now the only one of its kind left in circulation, following the demise of *Melody Maker* was, in its heyday, the de rigeur fashion accessory - in fact, before fashion accessories were invented - for any self-respecting male rock fan in the grey heydays of Classic Rock, the 1970s.

But now, thirty years and countless girl groups later, the *NME* has been magically transformed.

'What a band', Alex Needham had gushed in his piece on the group in the April 28th edition, 'a beacon of creativity and grace in a mainstream pop wilderness.' What would the traditional rock fan think of Destiny's Child? For many male forty-somethings, the attitude towards any music that departs from the hallowed formula of old - groups of former hod-carriers belting out mutated Muddy Waters tunes in a crowded pub - is that 'it's not real music'.

Compare the *NME*'s reverently pro-Destiny stance to that of the British 'quality' daily newspaper, *The Guardian*. 'Corporate R&B In Tinfoil Hotpants', declared Caroline Sullivan a few months earlier on Monday, November 20th 2000, in a review of the group's stage show at London Arena. 'Theirs is the sort of R&B where no single personality dominates. As long as the hits sound just like the records, the crowd wouldn't have cared if it had been three complete strangers on stage.' Does this mean that Destiny's Child are like a microwave ready meal - foil-wrapped and always the same? Then, on June 19th 2001, reviewing the group's triumphant appearance at Jam In The Park on the previous Sunday, a star-packed one-day R&B and hip-hop bash held in Finsbury Park on a typically cheerless British Summer's day, she wrote, 'the three Houston twenty year-olds are bulldozing their UK rivals. When Kelly thanks the audience for helping sell 5 million copies of *Survivor* in five weeks, 'she may as well have said, 'Atomic Kitten and Honeyz, give it up now'. At a time when real life seemed to be increasingly indistinguishable from 'reality' TV and all its bastard siblings, Destiny's Child constantly shame the competition by writing good songs, something we're not used to. Frankly, it seems that we no longer care what the music's like, so long as the singers' private lives are full of potential gossip.

Alexis Petridis, also writing in *The Guardian*, had stated, in his review of *Survivor* on April 27th, 2001 that 'the European pop clogging up the charts is regulated and uniform...it would be a shame if Destiny's Child became better known as a singing soap opera than a genuinely vital musical force.' In other words, with all their internal strife and its inevitable fall-out (there may be more to come, with the lawsuit against Mathew Knowles still pending), will they be able to survive the constant poking about in their collective emotional bottom drawer by the insatiable hunger of the public for more salacious bad news?

Miranda Saywer reckoned, in *The Observer*, June 24th, that 'you'd be forced to spear them with their own stiletto heels if they didn't make such brilliant music.'

So it seems that as soon as the hits stop coming, if they ever do, the knives will be out before you can say 'Christmas Album'. The world apparently waits with baited breath for them to make their first serious mistake.

In June, the group were subjected to an uncharacteristically negative response from the crowd at the Hot 97 Summer Jam, at which hip-hop's man of the moment, Jay-Z, invited Michael Jackson on-stage for a brief appearance, stunning the crowd in the process. Later, the audience roundly dissed Destiny's Child, booing after each song. Two weeks earlier at a National Basketball Association playoff game in Philadelphia, Michelle had been given an equally hard time for wearing a Los Angeles Lakers jersey, incensing the supporters of the Philadelphia home team, the 76ers. The group's publicist explained that the NBA had wanted the girls to show no partiality to either team, and between them they wore clothing supporting both sides, with Kelly giving it up for the 76ers, and Beyoncé representing the NBA and both teams. Still, it wasn't good enough and there were boos, boos, boos throughout their set. Some days even Destiny's Child just can't win. More awards nominations were announced in July, for the MTV Video Music Awards. The group was nominated in five categories two of which were for *Survivor* (Best Group Video and Best R&B Video). *Independent Women Part 1* was nominated for three awards - Best Pop Video, Best Video From A Film and Viewers Choice.

By this time the girls had embarked on the MTV TRL Tour, and were incorporating personal appearances in shopping malls up and down the country for the traditional 'signings'. A tour of the UK was announced for November, with promises of a musical extravaganza with plenty of surprises. On Sunday July 8th the group returned for another bash in another London park, this time a charity concert in Hyde Park for The Prince's Trust. Also on the bill were the UK group everyone loves to hate, Hear'Say, Sugababes (similarly), Geri Halliwell, Wyclef Jean, Shaggy, Ricky Martin, Craig David and Siscó, who spoilt everything by refusing to play his risque hit 'Thong Song'. As usual Destiny's Child stole the show, demonstrating the correct and proper way to perform high-class material before a paying audience, and shaming - as has become their custom - all other participants.

In the same month, Michelle discussed in interview her life in the group. Feeling now that she really was a permanent member (with all the revolving-door activity of the past eighteen months, she must sometimes have wondered), she had come to terms with her role as Beyoncé's and Kelly's partners. She would never be a lead singer, not at least in Destiny's Child, and she was resigned to that fact. Destiny's Child had saved her from her humdrum life as a backup singer: since joining the group her life had been a whirlwind of hotel rooms and work, work, work. Each song has its own dance routines, and with each tour the choreography has to be constantly developed, so that the old songs look new each time. On the eternal subject of any solo projects, she was emphatic that there would not be any, at least for the foreseeable future. Any spare time they had was spent in the studio, preparing for the next album, the often-rumoured Christmas collection that was, in fact, in preparation throughout the summer. But still, persisted the interviewer, who would you like to produce your solo album, even though you're not doing one? The reply was instant: 'Michael Jackson'.

The July 17th release of *Bootylicious* as a single gave the song several remix treatments. The regular CD version contained a 'V-Quest' treatment from Richard Vission, while the maxi single version also contained his dub version, and a mix by Big Boyz. The vinyl 12" version was expanded further, with the Big Boyz contributing an instrumental, along with the original album track and its own instrumental version.

CHAPTER TWELVE

DESTINY'S

CHILD

WHAT OF THE FUTURE?

Fast Forward - What Of The Future?

Advances in space technology during the 1960s and 70s gave the world several new toys to play with, including the digital media that now dominate the way we experience entertainment. The birth of the sampler in the early 1980s gave rise to the controversial growth of 'virtual' music. To the great delight of many do-it-yourself musicians, this meant you no longer needed a drummer, a bass player, or indeed anyone else at all except yourself, and as much digital gear as you could afford. No more tiresome guitar solos! No more vans breaking down! No more having to deal with the drummer's skanky girlfriend! In fact, very often, no more of anything except a driving beat and some spacey atmospherics. Add a drug - ecstasy - that focuses the mind on the repetitive nature of the music, and obviates the need for a 'performer' and you have a musical revolution on your hands. A generation is born for many of whom the idea of bands, with their inflated egos and an obsession with the dreary minutiae of their inner lives, is anathema. Clubbing becomes the new rock and roll, the dominant leisure pursuit for many millions all over the world, and the DJ, whose appearance is deliberately nondescript and whose presence onstage discreet to the point of near-invisibility, becomes the hero of the new revolution.

Sampling technology also gave rise, inevitably, to the idea of taking a well-known tune and remixing it, either with the artists' consent, in the case of legitimate DJ mixes, or without, in the case of 'bootleg' mixes or 'treatments'. Often these are then pressed up onto white-label vinyl, invariably with no information on the label, and distributed in relatively small quantities to the clubs, DJs and specialist shops.

Naturally the original artists are frequently ambivalent about this. Whilst recognising that to be bootlegged in this way may increase their credibility with hardcore clubbers and collectors, very few of these mixes achieve mainstream exposure. And, of course, the original artist isn't being paid. On a few notable occasions, bootlegs have been legitimised by the artist's record company via official release, raising the profile of both the original artist and the remixer. An example of this is 'Tom's Diner' by Suzanne Vega, released as a single in July 1987, whose bootleg mix by samplists D.N.A. subsequently became an official Top Twenty hit, and spawned an entire album of remixes.

Destiny's Child are not happy about bootleggers tinkering with their work, especially as it means that they see no money from it, they have no control over the quality, and that fans might mistake illegitimate releases for official product.

But the proliferation of peer-to-peer file sharing applications, where fans can download songs from each others' computers via the Internet, and the high-profile legal wranglings that Napster has become involved with, mean that the way we consume music has changed forever. While Napster and other sites like it may become regulated and enter into a pay-per-download system, fans will always seek out new ways of getting music free. Many musicians are offended by such apparent disloyalty, and their record companies are disturbed by the idea that so many sales are being lost.

There are already many unofficial remixes of Destiny's Child songs, and this is a trend that seems sure to become increasingly widespread as the technology becomes more widely available. It could be said that for a mainstream pop group to have its music reinterpreted by, for instance, an underground British drum and bass remix crew, as has been the case with two of Destiny's better-known songs, this is flattery indeed, though perhaps it is little consolation when they enjoy such great success on their own terms. However, the fact remains that hardcore fans will always want everything that bears the stamp of their heroes' names, whether officially sanctioned or not.

One of the more intriguing Destiny's Child collaborations is 'Thug Love', attributed to hip hop outfit 50 Cent, with Eminem and Redman. Beyoncé announces that a thug is what she wants, and needs, and that her friends don't understand. To say that hearing Destiny's Child in such a context comes a surprise is something of an understatement. When Caroline Sullivan wrote in *The Guardian* that to see Destiny's Child onstage at the Jam in the Park in June 2001 had made it seem as if they might as well be saying 'Atomic Kitten, give it up now', she could have had no idea how ironic her words would seem a month later. On the 29th July 2001, Atomic Kitten equalled Destiny's Child in having two consecutive UK Number One singles, when their cover of the Bangles' 'Eternal Flame' - itself originally an all-girl Number One - leapt straight to the top of the chart, repeating the success that their previous single *Whole Again* had achieved earlier in the year. Giving Beyoncé, Kelly and Michelle a straight run for their money, *Eternal Flame* kept *Bootylicious* at Number Two, though there was consolation in the fact that *Survivor* still held the Number One position in the album charts.

A few days earlier it had been announced that celebrations for Michael Jackson's grandiose 30th Anniversary celebrations, marking three decades of Jacko's presence at the forefront, more or less, of pop music, would include a performance by Beyoncé and the girls on the first of two concerts at Madison Square on September 7th 2001. Others sharing the bill would be Britney Spears, 'N Sync, Missy Elliott and Whitney Houston. It would be The King Of Pop's first performance in eleven years, and would be part of the intense marketing campaign for his new album, *Invincible*, rumoured to have cost a staggering 12 million dollars to record. Among the celebrities said to be lined up for the gala event was Marlon Brando, who would make a 'presentation', and word had also spread that the original Jackson 5 would reunite for the occasion, which was to be filmed for a two-hour TV special. For Destiny's Child, it would be the second opportunity to appear onstage with one of their childhood idols, the first having been the Divas 2000 spectacular almost a year previously, when they had performed with Diana Ross.

So by September 7th, 2001, Destiny's Child had gone full circle from the time they sat at home scrutinising videos of The Jackson 5 and The Supremes, avidly absorbing their style and technique. To perform at an event marking the extraordinary career of one of pop's most enigmatic superstars, in the company of so many celebrities of the past, present and no doubt the future, is itself a remarkable achievement for these young women who, barely three years previously, were nervously anticipating the release of their first album. They would seem now to have it all: their records, videos and styling now incorporate cutting-edge R&B, dance and fashion; it is seldom that their appearances onstage are received with anything less than an ecstatic response from their fans and critics alike, and sales of their third album look set to rival the achievement of the previous set, and may even surpass it.

Their generous gift of half a million hard-earned dollars to their local church, for the building of a recreation centre, showed that they really were prepared to put their money where their mouths were. Many celebrities forget pretty quickly where they have come from, and are only too pleased to get away. Beyoncé, Kelly and Michelle have always maintained that it is their faith that has kept them grounded, and, no matter what one may feel about their particular brand of religion, with its many declarations of being blessed and its insistence that their success is all part of God's plan, it is clear that something other than relentless ambition may have kept them bound to the timeless ethic of tireless hard work.

And with little having been heard of LaToya, LeTavia and Farrah since their hapless falls from grace, it would seem that for Kelly and Michelle, the best place to be is where they are now: in what is still one of the most successful bands on the planet.

increasing demands made on them by their fans, their management, their record company, and their own selves?

Perhaps it doesn't matter: they are all young enough to adapt, and they have time for their careers to evolve, in whatever shape or form they might take.

The Knowles Family empire seems certain to expand into an almost limitless universe of possibilities. There have already been Destiny's Child sponsored beauty products. Early on in the game, Mathew Knowles had used his expertise in the beauty industry to incorporate TV commercials to be run on local TV stations, featuring Destiny's Child promoting Soft and Beautiful Botanicals hair care. His sharp business acumen has seen the family business, which began with the humble hairdressing salon in Houston's Montrose Boulevard, expand into a formidable music management, marketing and production conglomeration, and it seems that it may only be a matter of time before Sony are relegated to the status of distributors for Mathew Knowles' label, Music World Music, as it broadens its interests wider than the soundtrack for *Carmen*, to include, at some point in the future, contractual obligations with Columbia notwithstanding, a release by Destiny's Child. With Beyoncé's sister Solange waiting for her own break as a solo artist, Mathew Knowles' presence on the music scene can only expand further.

And following Beyoncé's success in *Carmen*, it may not be long before finally Hollywood snaps her up for an acting role in a major blockbusting movie, which might see her presence in the group become increasingly marginalised. Even without the uncharitable comparisons with Diana Ross and her role in The Supremes, it is hard to escape the conclusion that Beyoncé is Destiny's Child, and that without her Kelly and Michelle would find themselves looking for employment elsewhere.

In the UK, the rapid rise of artists such as Craig David signals that the public's taste for sophisticated dance-based vocal music, call it what you will - soul, garage, or R&B - is still on the increase. Britain continues to produce world-class music, but its industry lacks the commitment to the sheer musical bravado displayed by American artists. It has, for instance, nothing to rival Steely Dan, who pride themselves on their flawless, old-school technique as musicians, and who, with *Two Against Nature* last year took two Grammys with an LP that came after a gap of twenty years, and who appeal to jazz, funk, rock and pop fans alike, young and old. With a rich musical heritage dating back in a continuous line to the birth of recorded jazz almost a century ago, Destiny's Child continue a tradition that has helped shape successive departures in form, encompassing everything from Louis Armstrong to Sisqó, and almost all points in between.

On the release of *Destiny's Child* in 1998, R&B was in a debilitated state. Three years later, and the songs blasting out of Destiny Central have made the genre almost unrecognisable. Their music has brought an indefatigable spirit, born of a healthy lust for life, fun and happiness, that their forerunners had either lost or had never known in the first place. It was as if Aretha Franklin's 'Respect' had leapt into a parallel universe, magically transformed into 'Independent Women', with all the guts and drive intact, and with no sign of the weariness and predictability that had infected R&B like some slow wasting disease.

Destiny's Child have crusaded against mediocrity, and have brought verve and colour to a scene that was gasping for breath. They have inspired countless other young wannabes, who will take their example and do as they have done, and may even surpass them. Whatever happens in the future, they have done what pop music is supposed to

DISCOGRAPHY

DESTINY'S

DISCOGRAPHY

CHILD

DESTINY'S CHILD
SURVIVOR
INCLUDES EXCLUSIVE REMIXES
destiny's child
Bootylicious
Includes CD Extra:
Bootylicious Video
Ed Case Remix
and a New
Bonus Track.
DESTINY'S CHILD

Discography

ALBUMS

Destiny's Child: *Second Nature / No No No Part II / Strange Games And Things / With Me Part I (Feat. JD) / Tell Me / Bridges / No No No Part I / With Me Part II (Feat. Master P) / Show Me The Way / Killing Time / Illusion (Feat. Wyclef Jean and Pras of Refugee Camp) / Birthday / Sail On / My Time Has Come (Dedicated To Andretta Tillman)*
CD - Columbia Records 1998

The Writing's On The Wall: *Intro (The Writing's On The Wall) / So Good / Bills Bills Bills / Confessions (Feat. Missy Elliott) / Bug A Boo / Temptation / Now That She's Gone / Where'd You Go / Hey Ladies / If You Leave (Feat. Next) / Jumpin' Jumpin' / Say My Name / She Can't Love You / Stay / Sweet Sixteen / Outro (Amazing Grace Dedicated To Andretta Tillman) Get On The Bus* - Also available with Limited Edition Bonus Disc featuring the tracks: *Independent Women Part I (Pasadena Remix) / Independent Women Part II / 8 Days of Christmas / No No No Part II (Feat. Wyclef Jean).*
CD - Columbia Records 1999

Survivor: *Independent Women Part I / Survivor / Bootylicious / Nasty Girl / Fancy / Apple Pie A La Mode / Sexy Daddy / Perfect Man / Independent Women Part II / Happy Face / Dance With Me / My Heart Still Beats (Feat. Beyoncé) / Emotion / Brown Eyes / Dangerously In Love / The Story Of Beauty / Gospel Medley (Dedicated To Andretta Tillman: You've Been So Good / Now Behold The Lamb / Jesus Loves Me / Total Praise / Outro (DC-3) Thank You.*
CD - Columbia Records 2001

SINGLES

No No No: *No No No Part 2 Featuring Wyclef Jean (Original Mix) / No No No (Instrumental) / No No No Part 1 / Second Nature*
CD - Columbia Records 1998

No No No: *No No No (Funki Dred Remix Featuring Wyclef Jean) / No No No (Funki Dred Remix feat. MCD) / No No No (Camdino Soul Extended Remix) / You're The Only One*
CD - Columbia Records 1998

No No No: *No No No Part 2 (Featuring Wyclef Jean) / No No No Part 1*
Vinyl 12" - Columbia Records 1998

With Me: *With Me Part 1 (Featuring JD) / With Me Part 1 (Featuring Master P) / Second Nature*
CD - Columbia Records 1998

With Me: *With Me (Full Crew Radio Version) / With Me (Full Crew Revocaled Version) / With Me (Full Crew Main Mix With Rap) / With Me (Full Crew Main Mix No Rap)*
CD - Columbia Records 1998

Get On The Bus: *Get On The Bus (Radio Version Featuring Timbaland) / Get On The Bus (Radio Edit Without Rap) / Illusions (Destiny Club Mix)*
CD - Columbia Records 1999

Bills Bills Bills: *Bills Bills Bills (Radio Edit) / Bills Bills Bills (Instrumental)*
CD - Columbia Records 1999

Bills Bills Bills Part 2: *Bills Bills Bills / Bills Bills Bills (Maurice's Xclusive Mix) / With Me (Part Ii)*
CD - Sony 1999

Jumpin Jumpin: *Jumpin Jumpin (Album Version) / Jumpin Jumpin (So So Def Remix) / Jumpin Jumpin (JD Remix, Featuring Jermaine Dupree, Da Brat and Lil Bow Wow) / Jumpin Jumpin (Maurice's Radio Mix) / Jumpin Jumpin (Azza's Radio Mix)*
CD - Columbia Records 2000

Say My Name: *Say My Name (Album Version Featuring Kobe Byrant) / Say My Name (Nitro Remix With Rap Featuring Nitro & Chief Of Mob Playas) / Say My Name (Maurice's Last Days of Disco Millennium Mix Instrumental) / Say My Name (Album Instrumental) / Say My Name (Nitro Remix Instrumental) / Say My Name (Maurice's Old Skool Dub Mix)*
Vinyl 12" - Columbia Records 2000

Say My Name: *Say My Name (Album Version) / Say My Name (Timbaland Remix)*
CD and Vinyl 12" - Columbia Records 2000

Bug A Boo: *Bug A Boo (Album Version) / Bug A Boo (Refugee Camp Remix) / Bug A Boo (Acappella) / Bug A Boo (Instrumental)*
CD - Columbia Records 2000

Independent Women Part 1: *Independent Women Part 1 (Album Edit) / Independent Women Part 1 (Acappella Version) / Independent Women Part 1 (Instrumental)*
CD - Columbia Records 2000

Survivor - The Dance Mixes: *Survivor (Calderone Club Mix) / Survivor (Calderone Drum Club Mix) / Survivor (CB 2000 Club Anthem Mix) / Survivor (Remix Extended Version Featuring Da Brat) / Survivor (Azza's Soul Remix)*
Vinyl 12" - Columbia Records 2001

Survivor - The Dance Mixes: *Survivor (Remix Extended Version Featuring Da Brat) / Survivor (Calderone Club Mix) / Survivor (Calderone Drum Club Mix) / Survivor (CB 2000 Club Anthem Mix) / Survivor (Azza's Soul Mix)*
CD - Columbia Records 2001

Bootylicious: *Bootylicious (Richard Vission's V-Quest) / Bootylicious (Richard Vission's DJ Dub) / Bootylicious (Big Boyz Remix) / Bootylicious (Big Boyz Remix Instrumental) / Bootylicious (Album Version) / Bootylicious (Album Instrumental)*
Vinyl 12" - Columbia Records 2001

Bootylicious: *Bootylicious (Album Version) / Bootylicious (Richard Vission's V-Quest)*
CD - Columbia Records 2001

Bootylicious: *Bootylicious (Album Version) / Bootylicious (Richard Vission's V-Quest) / Bootylicious (Richard Vission's DJ Dub) / Bootylicious (Big Boyz Remix) / Bootylicious (Case Remix)*
CD - Columbia Records 2001

RELEASES WITH OTHER ARTISTS

Sweet Kisses: *Woman In Me* - Destiny's Child and Jessica Simpson
CD - Sony/Columbia 1999

Thug Love: *Thug Love / I'm a Hustler* - Destiny's Child and Eminem under the name 50 Cent
CD Single - Sony/Columbia 2000

Try Again: *Try Again (Beatsmandes Mix) / Try Again (Real Mix)* - Destiny's Child with DMX and Aaliyah
CD Single - Sony/Columbia 2000

SOUNDTRACK ALBUMS

Men In Black: *Killing Time*
CD - Sony/Columbia 1997

Why Do Fools Fall In Love: *Get On The Bus*
CD - WEA/Elektra Entertainment 1998

Big Momma's House: *Big Momma's Theme* - Da Brat & Vita featuring Destiny's Child
CD - Sony/Columbia 2000

Romeo Must Die: *Perfect Man*
CD - EMD/Virgin 2000

Charlie's Angels: *Independent Women Part 1 / DOT*
CD - Sony Columbia 2000

Down To Earth: *Angel* (Kelly's solo single)
CD - Sony/Epic 2001

Carmen - MTV's Hip Hopera: *Survivor (Da Brat Remix) / Bootylicious (Rockwilder Remix, feat. Missy Elliott) / Cards Never Lie (Beyoncé Knowles with Wyclef Jean and Rah Digga) / If Looks Could Kill (You Would Be Dead) (Beyoncé Knowles with Mos Def and Sam Sarpong)*
CD - Sony/Columbia 2001

Child by Iris Gower
o 1999

Child: *The Unauthorized Biography In Words And Pictures* by Keith Rodway
ms 2001

Destiny: - CD Audio-Biography Plus Interviews
ms 2001

Child: Pop People by Eartha Glass
ade 2001

e: Destiny's Child
Services 2000

VIDEO AND DVD

Destiny's Child: *Survivor / Independent Women Part I (Live at the Brits 2001)*

DVD Single – Sony/Columbia 2001

The Platinums On The Wall: Collection of Destiny's Child Music Videos

VHS / DVD – Sony/Columbia 2001

ong the most comprehensive and a good place to start finding out about Destiny's Child online. Search eng
h as Yahoo and Google can uncover many more fan sites. Up-to-date information can also be found on ge
sic sites such as www.rollingstone.com, www.nme.com, www.mtv.com and www.getmusic.com.

EBSITES

ww.destinyschild.com - Official record company site

ww.dc-unplugged.com - Official fan club site

ww.absolutely.net/destiny/ - Great Destiny's Child photos

ww.ukbritney.tv/destinyschild/

ww.starpulse.com/Music/Destinys_Child

ww.angelfire.com/dc/zone/

tp://geocities.com/noconfessions/

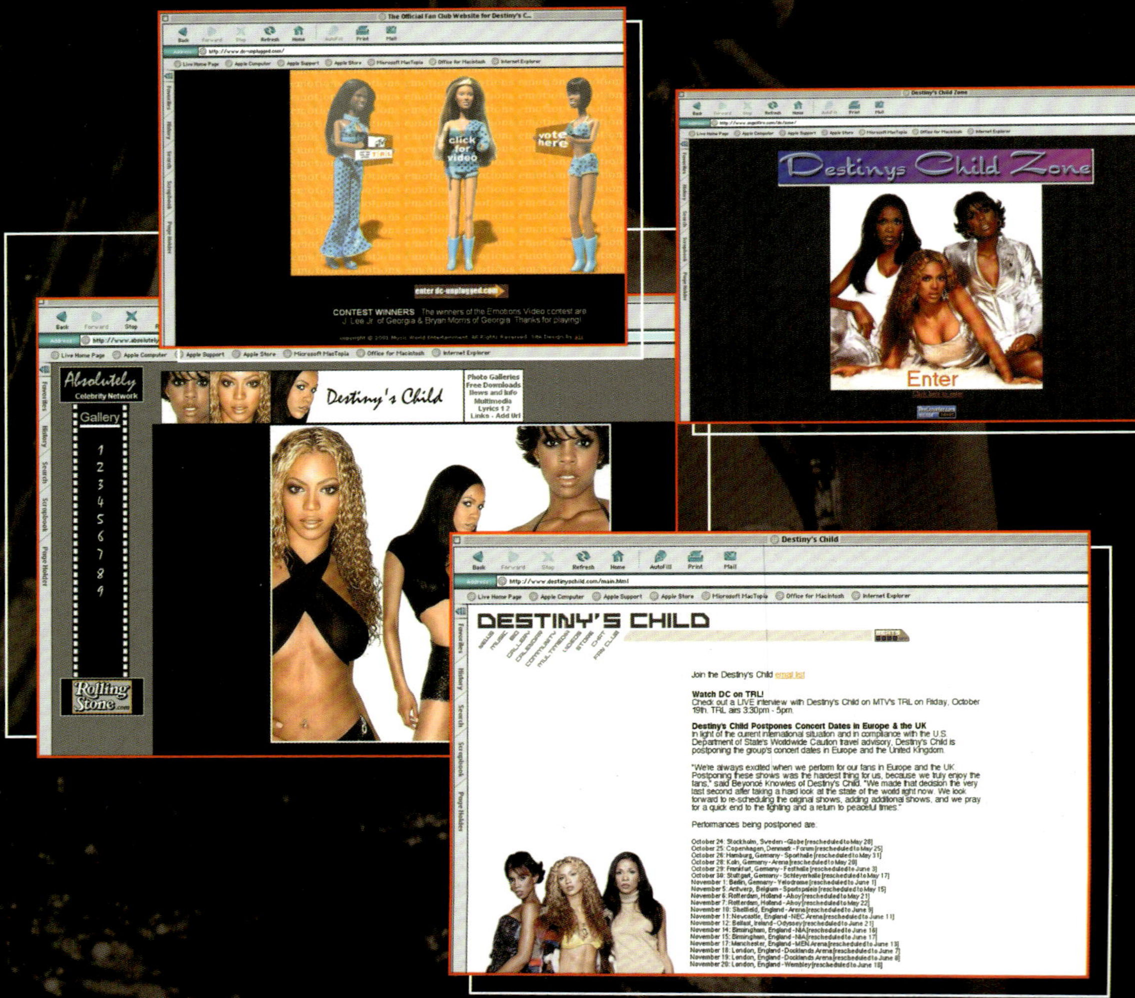

MP3s (Bootleg Mixes, Live Recordings and Unreleased Tracks)

Can't Help Myself - Unreleased track

Spilt - Unreleased track with Spiller Groovejet

Lady Marmalade - Unreleased studio demo

Cheerleading (Cheer Mix) - Destiny's Child and Jennifer Lopez

Ain't No Mountain High Enough - MTV live recording as Divas 2000, Destiny's Child with Mariah Carey, Diana Ross, Faith Hill, Donna Summer, Ru Paul.

No No No Scrubs (Coz Remix) - Destiny's Child vs. TLC

No No No (Megamenz Remix) - Destiny's Child with Wyclef Jean

No No No (Reggae Mix) - Destiny's Child vs. Beenie Man

Bills Bills Bills (Thunderpuss 2000 Remix)

Bills Bills Bills (Miami Latin Remix)

Bills Bills Bills (DJ Ken O.D. Drum & Bass Remix)

Bills Bills Bills (Destiny's Child & Sporty Thieves Trackmasters Remix)

Jumpin' Jumpin' (Mr E Remix)

Jumpin' Jumpin' (DJ Mixmaster Trax Remix) - Destiny's Child, Ja Rule, Def Squad

Jumpin' Jumpin' - Destiny's Child vs. It's Gonna Be Me

Say My Name (!2" Daddy D Remix)

Say My Name (UK Underground 2 Step Garage Mix)

Say My Name (DJ River's Dance Club Mix 2000)

Independent Women (Digital Beat Guru Remix) - Destiny's Child with Britney Spears

Stronger Independent Women (Digital Beat Guru Remix) - Destiny's Child with Britney Spears

Survivor (DJ Larry D Remix)

Bootylicious (DJ Dizney Remix)

Ooh Child, Things Are Gonna Get Better (live) - Destiny's Child with Cyndi Lauper

All Cried Out - Destiny's Child and 112

Medley: Independent Women/Jumpin' Jumpin'/Say My Name - Recorded live at the Billboard Music Awards, 2000

PHOTO CREDITS

Photos Courtesy of:

Sophia Reese

Redferns London

Pictorial Press London

Famous London

Rex Features London

Also Available From Chrome Dreams

Maximum Destiny

From the renowned Maximum series comes the complete and unauthorized biography on Destiny's Child incorporating:

- Newly researched biographical information
- Exclusive comments and interview material from Destiny's Child themselves
- Full-colour picture disc CD packaged with deluxe slipcase
- Free fold-out Destiny's Child poster
- Eight page illustrated booklet featuring rare photographs

Available from all good book and record shops or buy on-line at:

www.chromedreams.co.uk

Alternatively send a cheque or postal-order for £5.99 (£6.99 outside UK) to: Chrome Dreams, PO BOX 230, New Malden, Surrey KT3 6YY, UK.

Catalogue Number: ABCD093
ISBN: 1 84240 152 1